how to start a home-based

Interior Design Business, sixth edition

Other books in the How to Start series:

HOME-BASED BUSINESS SERIES

how to start a home-based

Interior Design Business, sixth edition

Revised by Linda Merrill

TAYLOR TRADE PUBLISHING
Lanham • Boulder • New York • London

Published by Taylor Trade Publishing

An imprint of The Rowman & Littlefield Publishing Group, Inc.

4501 Forbes Boulevard, Suite 200, Lanham, Maryland 20706

www.rowman.com

Unit A, Whitacre Mews, 26-34 Stannary Street, London SE11 4AB, United Kingdom

Distributed by NATIONAL BOOK NETWORK

British Library Cataloguing in Publication Information Available

Library of Congress Cataloging-in-Publication Data

Merrill, Linda, 1962–
  How to start a home-based interior design business / revised by Linda Merrill. — Sixth Edition.
     pages cm. — (Home-based business series)
  Summary: "Have you ever dreamed of starting your own home-based interior design business? Have you been hesitant to put your business plans into action? This book contains all the necessary tools and success strategies you need to launch and grow your business. An experienced designer shares her experiences and advice on every aspect of setting up and running a thriving home-based interior design business. Learn how to develop a business plan, estimate your start-up costs, price your services, and stay profitable once you're in business. Read all about getting clients and referrals, outshining the competition, bidding competitively, establishing your daily schedule, organizing your business, getting paid and much more. The book is packed with worksheets, including products and services charts, a sample balance worksheet, a profit-and-loss worksheet, a cash-flow projections worksheet, a weekly accounting ledger, a vendor sale sheet, and a bid sheet. "— Provided by publisher.
  Includes bibliographical references and index.
  ISBN 978-1-4930-0768-4 (paperback) — ISBN 978-1-63076-112-7 (electronic) 1. Interior decoration firms—United States—Management. 2. Home-based businesses—United States—Management. 3. Interior decoration—Practice. I. Title.
  NK2116.2.D48 2015
  747.068—dc23

                    2015000027

Printed in the United States of America

Contents

Introduction

Many experienced designers wish they'd had a blueprint when they first started their businesses. It would have kept them from making many mistakes and made the early years so much easier. Design schools teach the history and theory of design, but rarely how to run a business. This book was written to give you that advantage. In it you'll find all kinds of information on the business and how it works. You'll have access to elusive formulas and charts that new designers often have difficulty finding. In short, this book will give you the confidence and the knowledge to start a successful interior design business. So get comfortable, sharpen your pencils, and let's get started on making your dream of starting a home-based interior design business a reality!

01 | Design 101

Does your heart skip a beat when colors blend together perfectly? Does the concept of combining patterns excite you? Will you derive as much satisfaction from spending someone else's money and filling their home with beautiful and functional things as you would for yourself? If you answered yes to these questions, you may have the beginnings of what it takes to become a great interior design professional.

Of course, there is more to interior design than designing throw pillows and rearranging furniture. The business aspect cannot be ignored. You can be the most gifted, talented, and creative person in the world, but if you don't run your business wisely, you will not make it in this competitive field. This book provides the information that will help you set up and run a successful home-based interior design business. You'll have formulas and charts at your fingertips, providing you with the relevant information you'll need to get started in this fun and profitable business.

A start-up design business is a natural home-based business. Most of the sales take place in the customer's home because of the need to match color swatches to existing furniture or measure the windows for draperies. It is rare that a customer will ever have the need to come to your office. Of course, there are exceptions. As your business expands you may want to consider adding builders or commercial accounts to your list of clientele, and some may require that you have an office. (More about this later.)

The other good news about the design business is that there is always a demand for the services we provide. People will always buy new homes or remodel their old ones. In addition to that, the fact that this business can be started anywhere adds to the appeal. The design companies that market themselves as product-driven companies have an even greater advantage. For example, when a person moves into a new home, he or she may not be able to afford a "designer" (or is possibly nervous about losing control) but will definitely need new window coverings and maybe carpet, or perhaps have a sofa that needs to be reupholstered. There are ample opportunities to market our services to be the most appealing to specific types of clients, from those looking for whole-home remodels and decorations to more targeted purchases such as windows or floors. These various marketing techniques will be covered in the advertising chapter.

What Are Your Options?

The design field is multifaceted. There are many types of occupations, each doing a very different and specific job. Your first step will be to determine where you want your area of focus, or expertise, to be. First, let's discuss the differences between a decorator and a designer. This question actually causes more arguments in the field than any other and the answer varies greatly depending on who is answering the question. It is important to note that for the purposes of this book, we are mainly referring to residential design and decor and not commercial projects, though there is some crossover. In very broad terms, a decorator's focus is primarily on the surface materials of a space and a designer's focus is both surface materials as well as the functional use of a house and all the services that support the functional use. It varies state by state, but certain education, accreditation, licensing, and registrations (known as *Title Acts* or *Legislation*) may be required in order to call oneself an interior designer or even market your services as "design" services. It's important to know what your specific region's requirements are.

Interior designers who have received American Society of Interior Designers (ASID) certification must have achieved a certain level of education, have worked in the field for a number of years, and then pass an exam (National Council for Interior Design Qualification [NCIDQ]). Much of the focus on this level of certification includes deep understanding of commercial design, which includes hospitality, healthcare, educational, and business settings. Because these are public spaces involving health and safety issues, a deep level of knowledge is needed to create proper design plans and then implement them. Since we are primarily focused on residential design, it's safe to say that in most cases, a decorator is generally just as well received in the public eye as a designer. Quite frankly, the only people who know the difference between a designer and a decorator are the people working in the field. For simplicity, we will use the title of *designer* throughout this book, which will refer both to someone offering general interior design consulting services as well as product-driven sales occupations.

When starting an interior design business, you should decide if you are going to focus on being a product-driven designer or a design consultation–driven designer. A product-driven designer may choose to sell a specific line or lines of products (or antiques, for instance) as a way to gain entree into a client's home and then also be able to provide additional design services as need arises. A consulting designer markets his or her design consulting services around creating an overall design plan for a single room or an entire home and then may or may not also sell the homeowners the products. The following questions may help you decide.

Do you like really getting in there and getting your hands dirty? If a drapery is hanging wrong, would you climb a ladder and straighten it out or would you call an installer to do it for you? If you would climb the ladder yourself, you would do well as a hands-on, product-driven designer.

If a client called you to buy just one shade for her new home, would you consider taking the job? If you consider small jobs a gateway to larger ones, you will do well as a product-driven designer.

Do you love reading technical specifications and keeping up on all the latest product news in a specific product field? If so, focusing on this field and truly becoming an expert may be a great way for you to break into the business.

Do you have the ability to "see" a finished space fully realized in your head? If so, you will likely be happier working on an entire space versus pieces and parts.

Can you juggle many different vendors and product details while knowing when to bring in experts in areas you need help with? Knowing one's strengths and weaknesses and still bringing the best final result to the client is the hallmark of a great design consultant.

Can you establish a long-standing relationship with clients, nurturing their business over long periods of time, sometimes years? If so, then a career as a consultative designer is a good fit for you.

If you would rather sell lots of product to lots of clients, you may wish to focus on product lines. If, however, the thought of having a small number of big clients is appealing, you may prefer the consulting route.

Do you feel comfortable selling yourself and your expertise or will you find it easier to sell a specific product? A design consultant is selling themselves and their ideas and it takes a good amount of self-confidence to do that.

Product-Driven Designer

If you do feel that selling yourself and your expertise seems the more difficult route to go, bringing in product lines may be the best choice for you, especially at the outset. In this type of business, you are marketing the products more than the design services. While a sales job may well turn into a design job, a large portion of your income will be derived from product sales.

In this type of business, the designer may advertise various products and offer free design advice if the client purchases all the products from her or him. There are decent markups on most of the products, so it is well worth your time if you handle it right. However, it must be noted that it's very easy for clients to "shop" you both in other stores and online. Offering too much free advice can result in giving away your ideas and not making the sale. In fact, you've sold the clients on the product, but they may not buy it from you. It is very important to limit the time spent in the customer's home with a prearranged agreement and charge a per-hour fee if the customer requires more time. You can always offer additional time as you feel is warranted, but start with a more strict policy so the client knows the parameters of the arrangement. Another way to make sure you do not waste your time is to let your customers know that if they buy the product from someone else after you have spent time with them, they are obligated to pay you a predetermined design fee. Of course, if you're selling products in small quantities, these concepts are less important. But if you're working on a large project, you could be into it for hours of your time and end up with nothing to show for it.

Design Consultant

If you choose to market yourself as a design consultant, or a consultation-only designer, an interior design degree is helpful though not necessarily needed (unless required in your region as discussed previously). As a new design consultant, it can be difficult to attract clients as you may have no portfolio or references, but you have to start somewhere. It is more difficult to succeed as a consultant because you are not selling any products, just your expertise, which is an intangible. It's easier to advertise a "SALE" on blinds than a sale on your expertise. A training option for those who want to have this type of business is to spend time working at a high-end furniture store or an upscale design shop gaining experience. Regardless of your age, don't hesitate to take a design internship with an established firm. While unpaid internships are generally frowned upon, a low-wage internship, or job shadowing, will help you gain important insight in how to run a consulting firm from establishing trade accounts (fabric, furnishings, lighting, and more) and maintaining a design library for your samples to working with construction trade. Nothing beats hands-on experience and even design schools don't teach the everyday processes of running your own business.

Residential or Commercial?

While this book is primarily focused on residential design, there is a certain amount of potential crossover. Even so, you need to decide which client you want to target more aggressively. If you decide to cater to residential clients, you will surely design the homes of business owners and managers, which may lead to commercial jobs.

Generally, residential jobs are smaller in size but reap a higher profit margin than commercial projects. You are working directly with the homeowner, and many close relationships and even friendships are formed this way. You will be working with small details, such as designing place mats to coordinate with the kitchen valance you've just hung, to large details, such as selecting cabinets and appliances.

Commercial jobs are usually not that intimate. The retail prices of the jobs are higher, but there is a substantially lower profit margin. If you are designing the bedspreads and draperies for a hotel, more than likely the rooms will all look the same, so after choosing the fabric, it's just a matter of taking measurements and working up a bid.

Because there is much crossover between product-driven and consultative designers, this book is focused toward product sales as the driver of one's business, but will include consulting-only information as well.

Working with Builders

A great source of referrals and income for any type of designer are builder accounts.

There are two ways that working with builders can bring you business: (1) model home design, and (2) new homeowner color and finishes selections. A builder usually wants a track record from a designer before assigning these projects. The following points briefly describe the ins and outs of this type of work.

1. **Model home design.** There is not a lot of money to be made decorating models, but indirectly it can pay well. A builder sets aside a decorating budget for each model home that he or she builds. An experienced builder or developer will understand the value that the design brings to the project and will set aside sufficient budget for the designer to best showcase the property. The designer's job is to produce a great result within the limits of the budget. It's not the emotional process that working with a homeowner can be; the builder isn't interested in how pretty this fabric is versus that fabric. There will be times when the budget isn't really sufficient and the designer will spend many hours figuring out how to finish the job by calling in favors and borrowing furnishings. In any event, it is a time-consuming process as the designer is also expected to attend many meetings and walk-throughs with the builder. Yet the competition for

model home design work is fierce as there is a fair amount of recognition that stems from decorating a model (make sure that your company name will be posted on signs throughout the house and that you can leave your business cards and brochures). If the model is part of a large high-end luxury apartment or homeowners complex, all the future homeowners will have seen your work on display.

2. **Finish and appliance selections.** When people buy a new home while it's under construction, they must pick out lighting, carpet, flooring, wallpaper, brick, indoor and outdoor paint, appliance colors, tile, and a roof, plus lots more! Larger, more experienced builders usually bring in a designer to help the customer with these decisions as it can help keep the project on track. While your fee for this service may not be huge, it gets you in the door at a crucial point in the design/build process. The designer has the first shot at getting the customer's business for window coverings, furniture, or the entire design of the house.

Lucrative Extras

One very important area of design is space planning and it's not necessarily a builder's forte. Offer your client, whether it is the builder or homeowner, your expertise in planning the home to better benefit the client's needs. You can check floor plans for areas that may need to be changed to create a better flow or easier access and adequate storage. Perhaps it's the placement of light fixtures or whether the client wants a single or double vanity sink in the master. These are a couple of the many decisions that need to be made and it saves everyone money and time if they are made before the work begins. Also let your client know, as part of space planning, that you can provide furniture arrangements and whatever other products or services you offer. Clients that may be relocating and bringing furniture with them often appreciate this service very much. They may be uncertain how specific pieces will fit into their new floor plan.

What Does a Designer Do?

Merriam-Webster's Collegiate Dictionary defines an interior designer as "a person whose job is to plan how the rooms of a building should be furnished and decorated." It's true, an interior designer does design a space, but there is a lot more that happens behind the scenes to get a business off the ground and keep it up and running. This book will cover all of the areas in detail, but here are some of the basic elements of business ownership.

Marketing

You will be responsible for crafting your brand image and marketing your company. This starts with creating your company name and making decisions on how you wish to get the word out about your products and services. Will you be paying for advertising or doing a lot of personal networking? Unless you are personally well-funded or can trade services with a graphic designer, you will be creating your own ad layouts, brochures, even business cards. You will be designing and building a website, or hiring someone to do it for you. Your job will include regular updates to your online presence and print prices to reflect changes in your product offerings, services, awards received and new projects completed. More on this in chapter 6.

Client Relations

- Good clients are worth gold and need to be nurtured throughout the life of the project and into the future. They are the source of ongoing business as their own needs change and evolve, and they are the best source of referrals to new clients. Larger clients may receive more attention than smaller ones, but all should feel valued and appreciated in some way.

- You will have to learn how to budget your time with each customer to avoid turning a sales call into a social hour or allowing them to take advantage of you by asking for additional "free" advice while in their home. At times, you will be looked upon as a friend, confidant, and even marriage counselor. Do this well and you become a trusted resource, but being too cozy can be time consuming without the appropriate payoff.

- One of the most frustrating aspects of the job is the irate and unsatisfied customer. Sadly, it's bound to happen at some point and you may have no control over the situation. Since yours is a custom business, it is inevitable that you will have some problems. For instance, you may be manufacturing a pair of custom draperies for a client's home, and it is important to the client that the draperies are installed by Christmas, which is five weeks away—just enough time to get the job done. When you place the order, you verify that there is enough fabric in stock to complete the job. You put the file away and wait for the draperies to arrive. Two and a half weeks later, you receive a postcard in the mail from the manufacturer explaining that there was a flaw in the fabric and the new fabric has been ordered from the mill; your new delivery date for the goods is January 15. It will be your responsibility to call your customer and explain that not only will the draperies not be ready in time for the holidays, but it's now too late to choose another fabric. If handled well, most customers will be disappointed but accepting of the situation. But some will be upset and you will receive the brunt of it. If you have a problem dealing with situations like this, you might want to rethink your career decision, because such glitches are not uncommon.

Office Management

- You will be setting up trade accounts and working with the sales representatives to establish your discounts on products. You will be constantly bombarded with new products, and you will have to decide what you will and will not sell in your business and keep track of all your resources.

- You will have to find the time to keep all the products updated in your library, brochures and website. Things change fast in this business, and if you sell a product that has been discontinued or has had a significant price increase, it will be embarrassing to explain to your client that you had not gotten around to updating your files and samples.

- You will be creating estimates and invoicing your clients, collecting their deposits and balances at the appropriate times. You also will be the bill collector in the event that one of your clients refuses to pay. In addition to the small aspects of bookkeeping, you will be responsible for the overall record keeping of your business, including taxes and licensing as required by your local region.

Design

- While we all go into this business for the love of the actual design work, it's still work. A successful designer will be able to understand their client's needs and desires, even if they aren't clearly expressed. As the professional, you are obligated to bring the best level of design work to the project, while also giving the clients what they want. If what they want isn't appropriate for a given situation, you will need to be able to bring them to understanding and approval. You will have to be a salesperson in every sense of the word. Not only will you have to be talented in design, you also will have to be able to convey your ideas to customers in a way that will make them want to buy. But ultimately, it's their house and you should not try to make clients take something they don't want. It takes patience and observation, which grows with experience.

- There will be times when you will have to work up numerous presentations until you find the one that your client likes enough to buy. However, in order to be profitable, you will need to keep tight control on how much time is spent in the design and shopping phase of the project so that it's in keeping with the design fee you have charged. If you're charging a flat fee for the project, you may wish to limit the number of options you provide the client before additional fees kick in. If you're billing by the hour, then as long as the client doesn't mind paying for your time, it may be okay to show numerous options. Over time you will develop a process that works best for you. In any event, you will want to clearly outline your process and charges in a letter of agreement that the client has signed off on.

Implementation

- You will be the scheduler and rescheduler for all of your design appointments. You will also have to oversee work crews, including window covering installers, carpet layers, wallpaper hangers, carpenters, electricians, and more.

- You will be responsible for mapping out a room, taking measurements for draperies or flooring, and sometimes (in a pinch) even doing simple installations.

- You will have to work up bids on each job and estimate the materials needed for each product.

- You will have to order all the materials needed for a job from each manufacturer. Your profit margin lies in your ability to order exactly the right amount of product for a given job. Order too much and you've overpaid for unused goods that you might be throwing into your sales bin; order too little of, say, a fabric for window treatments, and you may not be able to complete the job, which is a disaster for you and your client.

- You will have to log in each product as it's received and then check it for flaws, missing parts, and color variations. If you are using a workroom for your upholstery or window treatments, you will want to be sure they know what fabric is coming for each job by providing them with a sample so they can do this rigorous check-in. If there are problems such as flaws or misshipments, you will have to work with the vendor to get replacements quickly as well as reschedule any trades people involved and communicate any delays to your client.

- It will be your responsibility to make sure the fabric gets to the workroom, the wallpaper gets to the right house, or your vacationing client's home is open for the work crews on a Saturday or Sunday. And sometimes you will act as the delivery person yourself when needed.

- You will be doing all the invoicing, collecting, and paying bills, or if you hire a bookkeeper, you will need to be overseeing his or her work. You are required to collect sales tax per your local laws and remit same to your department of revenue on a timely basis. You will need to be fully insured and, where required, registered as a general contractor if you are managing work crews.

Required Assets and Traits for the Job

Although the world of interior design is a challenging, fulfilling career, it takes a unique individual to rise to the challenges that are encountered every day in this job. Here are some important traits that help in running a successful interior design business. Be honest with yourself as you read through them, because each one is vitally important to this career.

- **Self-esteem.** You will run into many obstacles, especially when just starting your business. Real estate agents will tell you no, you will lose bids to competitors, contractors will ignore your requests, and customers will be disappointed with your work. It's essential to have an attitude that will allow you to dust yourself off after disappointments and keep going.

- **A good support group.** If you are married, it's important that your spouse (and children, if you have them) back up your decision to go into business for yourself. There will be evenings when you work all night to meet a deadline and if you don't get support, it will be hard to keep motivated. If you are not married and don't have children, make sure your friends and family are aware that at times you will need their support and understanding.

- **Patience.** As a designer, you will come across many situations that test your patience. A customer will remember a fabric being just a shade bluer, or someone will take up hours of your time, probing your mind for ideas, then decide not to buy anything. Such aggravation is just part of the job.

- **Organization.** Because of the many details you will be handling at any given moment, organization is key. You will hopefully have several jobs going on at one time, and you must keep track of the progress of all of them and keep them moving forward.

- **Motivation.** Your alarm clock will be your only boss in the morning. No one will tell you to go out and market your business or to be on time to your appointment. You must be a self-starter and self-disciplined in order to be successful in a home-based business.

- **The ability to listen.** To be a good designer and salesperson, you must be able to listen to the client's needs—only then can you fill them. For example, some customers already know exactly what they want and can communicate their thoughts clearly. But often, you will have to listen carefully to what the client says and even doesn't say in order to be successful and help them achieve their desired results.

- **Authoritativeness.** A designer will be in charge of all aspects of a job, including the installation. You will have to supervise numerous workers during the course of the day. There will be times when your drapery installer has a different vision than yours about the way a pair of draperies needs to be hung, and you will have to make the authoritative decision. You are always your clients' advocate and are working on their behalf. You can't back down to a tradesman or workroom if you know you are right.

- **You don't get easily flustered.** A steady temperament will help you deal with a business filled with daily crises and successes.

- **Interest in people.** Regardless of whether you deal in residential or commercial jobs, you will be in constant contact with people. Some will change their minds on a continual basis and call you ten times a day. This is all part of the job, so if you don't like people—that is, if you aren't a "people person"—then this may not be the career for you.

- **Math skills.** You will use basic math daily. Ordering carpet, blinds, fabric, wallpaper, and window treatments will require you to do some basic calculations to determine proper sizes and amounts to order. Keep your tape measure and calculator handy and never hesitate to have an installer or workroom check your numbers—two pairs of eyes are better than one!

- **Never stop learning.** The desire to keep up on trends as well as understanding historical design styles is all-important, as is keeping up on legal issues and product information. Be open to new ideas and seek out inspiration.

The Myths and Realities of Entrepreneurship

Before we discuss the details of setting up your business, let's examine your motives for wanting to be self-employed. You have your own reasons for wanting to be your own boss, as does everyone else who wants to try it. The following list contains some of the misconceptions that are associated with self-employment.

MYTH: No one will tell you what to do; you are the boss.

REALITY: Every one of your customers will be your boss. Remember the old adage that says the customer is always right? When operating a small business, that is the golden rule—along with writing a good contract and keeping your terms of service clear and understandable. You want to give your customer what they want, but you need to protect yourself against being taken advantage of. Word of mouth or referral business is absolutely the best business you can get. If you have an unhappy customer, you would be surprised how fast word will spread around the neighborhood and online (and among that person's co-workers, friends, and family, and lots of people they don't even know). On the other hand, a satisfied customer will offer personal recommendations, which are golden.

MYTH: Your time will be your own.

REALITY: While there is great flexibility, there is no one to pass your work on to when you're tired or have other plans. To use an old cliché, the buck stops with you. If you have a proposal to work up on the weekend of a family campout, you have to make a choice. The design fairy refuses to work alone while you and your family are playing!

MYTH: You will become instantly rich.

REALITY: Although it is possible to make an excellent income running your own business, it will not happen overnight. Some businesses take years to even turn a profit. If you're running a product-driven business, you will likely have had to invest heavily in samples to showcase your wares. It can take a long time to recoup the initial outlay of cash and start turning a profit. A design consulting service grows slowly, client by client, and it can take a while to learn how to charge appropriately for profitability.

MYTH: You won't have to work as hard as you do when working for someone else.

REALITY: Because you are the only one responsible for your business, you will have to work twice or three times as hard as you would working a 9-to-5 job. You may only have to go on two appointments a day to make your required income, but there is much to be done besides selling the product. If this is one of your misconceptions, please refer back to the basic job description.

MYTH: Interior design is so glamorous!

REALITY: If you've been reading up to this point, you will have gotten a glimpse into a very unglamorous side of the business. Yes, sometimes there is glamour, but that's maybe 10 percent of your time. Most of the time, it's details, details, details; the client's dirty laundry to be stepped over; and dirty footprints on newly installed carpets that you yourself may be cleaning.

A Few Loose Ends

Most people jump right in when starting a new home-based business, and the road to success inevitably becomes harder than it has to be. You are taking an excellent positive step by reading this book, but to ensure your success, don't quit your day job quite yet, and do follow these guidelines.

If you can save three (preferably six) months of living expenses, you will be way ahead of the game. If you have the time (or patience), start saving long before you plan to open your new business. This may eliminate the need to apply for a small business loan; such loans are nearly impossible to get for new, untested businesses, especially home-based ventures.

If you need a car or to refinance your mortgage, do it while you still have a paycheck. Most financial institutions will loan you money only if you have a steady paycheck coming in.

If you have health insurance, plan to continue it through the Consolidated Omnibus Budget Reconciliation Act (COBRA) or one of the newly formed health exchanges. If you can get on a spouse's policy, do so. Do the same thing with your life insurance policy and investigate disability insurance.

In summary, there are many advantages to being employed when you make the decision to go into business for yourself. Plan your launch carefully and keep a steady paycheck for as long as possible, until you know the time spent at your "old job" is infringing on your ability to move forward.

Testing the Waters

So you love the thought of interior design. Perhaps, even after reading this far in the book, you are still enchanted with the idea. Then test it. This may be the hardest suggestion to swallow, but it's also one of the most important. Even a person who has been in the design field for many years doesn't know everything about this business—it's just impossible.

To further your chances of success, you may want to spend a little time working for an established design firm or store that offers design services. You may learn what regions or towns have the best clients and thus where to focus your marketing in the future. It also will give you a chance to work with and become comfortable with the different products and manufacturers and allow you to gain experience that will give you practical knowledge in the design field. When first starting out in this complicated business, you are sure to make costly mistakes. Being employed and trained by someone else will soften the blow on your pocketbook throughout the learning curve. Make sure that you train with a company that does not require you to sign a noncompete agreement (see chapter 10 for further explanation) as part of your employment.

Determining Your Level of Participation

This business can be run on a part-time or full-time basis, depending on how much time you want to devote to it. Obviously, the more you work, the more money you will make. Even part-time interior design is a time-consuming business. If you decide to go into it full time, be prepared to work a minimum of ten to twelve hours a day. In the beginning that time will be devoted to establishing your processes, deciding on products to sell, and networking and marketing your services. Over time, you will spend many hours a day doing client work, and keeping up with all of the back-end processes. But you will have more flexibility than most jobs. Because you are in control of your schedule, you can pencil in a dentist appointment and a lunch date without having to ask anyone.

If You Have Children

Ask any parent what they want more of and the answer you'll likely get is time. So how can a parent of a small child possibly run a business out of his or her home? The answer is simple: structure and planning. You may have to get up earlier in the morning to figure a bid or stay up late at night to go through fabric swatches for a presentation in the morning, but if you are willing to schedule your day, and stick to it, you should be able to squeeze out a few more hours. Paperwork and phone orders can be taken care of during the day, during nap time, for instance.

Day care is another option, either limited or on a full-time basis. If you're uncomfortable with leaving your child at a day-care facility, consider bringing a babysitter into your home. By closing yourself up in your office with a "disturb only in an emergency" mentality, you can be quite productive. Don't forget about any nearby relatives—they can be invaluable in a deadline situation.

Be sure to include your children in your work, rather than totally excluding them. If they know that work time is fun because they get to do "paperwork" or open mail, they won't resist or automatically demand attention every time you sit down to work. And that goes not just for little kids but also spouses, friends, and parents. Those who don't work from home sometimes forget that, though we may be sitting at our kitchen tables in our bunny slippers, we're still working—or should be. They will need to be trained to treat your work time with the same respect that they did when you worked for another company.

Read, Read, Read

There are quite a few informative trade magazines that offer a wealth of information. In addition to interior design magazines, there are specific ones dealing with products such as window coverings, carpet, wood flooring, and more. It is to your advantage to subscribe to and read these periodicals on a monthly basis. They will keep you updated on new products and will give you ideas about how to make use of the existing ones. In the appendix in the back of the book, you will find resources, trade associations, and periodicals that should help get you started.

Associations

There are a number of associations connected to the design field that will increase your knowledge as well as give you possible leads for your business. Some of the associations you may want to look into are:

- **Builders Associations.** These are organizations that consist of builders working in a particular geographic area. This is also a good place to make business contacts for possible design referrals and for your own resource list. Builders Association chapters typically hold meetings and have social functions. There is a yearly fee required to join; check with your local association for specific information.

- **The Board of Realtors.** This organization is made up of real estate agents who also have a constant need for interior design help, whether they know it or not. For example, when an agent is representing a client who is selling a home, they may need new carpet or window coverings to make the home more marketable. That's where you come in. The agent has to feel confident in her recommendation, and once you build a relationship with her by doing a few quality jobs, the referrals will start coming with more frequency. The key to this association is to network, pass out your cards, and ask for business. If you do quality work at reasonable prices, the word will get around.

- **Chambers of commerce, small business associations, and countless others.** The more associations you join, the more networking you will do, and the more business you will gain. The wonderful thing about this business is that everyone, at one time or another, will need your services, particularly window coverings. Join as many associations as you have time for and can afford. It's a great way to market your business. Be sure to look online for associations in your specific area.

Further Your Education

If you don't already have a degree in design, you may consider obtaining an associate's degree in interior design at a local community college or working toward a certificate in design, which may be offered at a local school of design or architecture. Real education cannot be overvalued and is a great confidence booster. Some other courses you might consider are accounting, taxes, marketing, and basic business classes. In addition to these, manufacturers put on seminars specifically planned for the design business, such as how-to's for the various products, installation guidelines, and tips for up-selling to more expensive products. Keep in touch with local distributors and design centers and get on their mailing lists for these events.

Be Prepared

If this chapter has taught you anything, it is to be prepared before opening your business. When taking the leap from working for someone else to being your own boss, your road to success will be much less bumpy if you are prepared. Be realistic with yourself, and if you know of an area that you're weak in, work on it or possibly hire someone who can help you. Remember, the more you can plan while still on someone else's payroll, the better off you will be when you take that final, exciting step toward your new independent lifestyle.

Setting Up Shop

Among the many benefits of running a business from your home is that your office will be located approximately one minute from your bedroom. This can work either for or against you. You must be self-motivated to work out of your home because the distractions will be numerous: Your children will want your full attention, your spouse will expect you to run errands in your "spare time," your friends will call daily wanting to gossip, the remote control will entice you, and your house will probably never be cleaner. (Giving in to such distractions is commonly known as *procrastination*.) If you are a self-motivated person, as I suspect you are if you are still reading, you can overcome these obstacles.

The first thing you should do is set up your work space. It must be an area that is dedicated solely to your business. When you walk into this space, whether it's an entire room or a partitioned-off section of a larger room (i.e., the living room), you are at work. This concept needs to be understood by your family members, friends, and, most importantly, you.

Interior design is a business of details, and you must be equipped to handle them. It would be ideal if you have an extra study or a bedroom that you can convert into an office, but if not, a partitioned section of your living room, kitchen, or garage will do for starters. You need to take into consideration your individual needs. If you have children or other responsibilities, you need to keep that in mind when determining your office setup.

Peace and quiet is something that should be considered when choosing your office space, so be sure to consider the noise level of the area as well as the traffic volume. You will be speaking on the telephone and working on complicated bids that take a tremendous amount of concentration.

What You'll Need

The items you need in your office are basic. Some people make the mistake of going to the office supply store and spending a bundle; there is no need to. When first opening a business stick to the basics and keep your expenditures as low as possible. Use the bulk of your start-up capital for more important things, such as samples and advertising (the projected start-up cost worksheet in chapter 3 will help you plan more effectively). Here is a list of necessities:

- **Desk, filing cabinet, and storage cabinet.** You can usually find these at a secondhand store or a discount office store reasonably priced. You will need space to store product samples, forms, and miscellaneous office supplies.

- **Basic office supplies.** This includes paper, pens, paper clips, standard and expandable file folders, message pads, calculators (desktop and portable), a briefcase or carryall for appointments, and a mobile smart phone.

- **Computer.** You will need a dedicated computer with high-speed internet access (desktop or laptop) to keep track of your jobs, estimating, and billing; keep up on who owes you and whom you owe; and perform your overall bookkeeping. More and more, vendors are hosting their catalogues and brochures online, so quick and easy online access is imperative. Do not use a shared computer with family. You are running a professional business and this is a must-have item and a definite "basic" in today's world. As a side note: Never share an email address with a family member. Your email address should reference your company name or your own name or should come from your website URL. Anything else is unprofessional.

- **Telephone.** Establish a dedicated phone number and line for your business. Many are forgoing the landline altogether and using a cell phone so they are on top of calls wherever they are. Don't use a family line as this will always look less than professional—especially if one of your kids should answer it or pick up another extension while you're on a business call. Even though we are working from home, we need to be as professional as possible. That you're at home should be an invisible part of your operation. When you answer your business phone, you should answer in a professional manner, stating the name of your business. Your voicemail message should be professional and you should check it regularly so that you can return calls promptly. A quick call return can make the difference between a $10 or a $10,000 day.

- **Fax machine.** Though many vendors and companies have online systems to take orders or accept orders via email, the fax machine is still an important tool for most offices. Aside from the time savings, written orders have a paper trail of what was ordered so that you can check it against deliveries. Calling in orders can result in mistakes that cost real money. It's best to get a combo fax/printer/scanner to cover all your needs.

■ **Forms and documents.** Most forms today are electronic and can be printed as needed. However, some vendors do still require the use of their preprinted forms, so you will need to have a place to store these if needed.

■ **Tape measure.** While this should be obvious, it's the tool that will always be your number one for every job you do and everything you sell. Most of the items measured will be taken to $\frac{1}{8}$ inch so invest in a good, strong steel tape measure that is easy to read in low-level lighting situations and doesn't crinkle when fully extended. Most designers actually have different types of tape measures for different needs such as a small, pocket-size one to carry around at all times up to the kind that contractors use (more about this in chapter 9).

■ **Business cards, letterhead, and envelopes.** These things are all wise investments for any business. When you send out correspondence, you want to project a professional image, and you will need business cards in many situations. These are a form of advertising for your company and should be the best you can afford. On a side note, your business card information should also be your email "signature" that is attached to the bottom of all your emails. It should include your name, your full business name and tag line if you have one, address and phone, and website and social media links. Every email you send is an opportunity to put your name in front of other people; it's free and professional looking.

■ **Digital Camera.** You will want to start a portfolio that includes your best jobs as soon as you can. These days, most designers' portfolios are part of their websites and it's rare to have a printed portfolio. But, some customers may request to see your work in printed form, so it's best to be prepared. While it's preferable to have a professional photographer shoot your work, it's not always possible in the early stages of a business. If you're taking your own photos, it would be well worth the small investment to take a photography course at a local adult-ed program or college. Always shoot your photos in good light with the high-resolution setting for optimal results. Your phone likely has a camera on it as well, and this is fine for quick product or furniture snaps but will never be good enough for your portfolio. The quality of your photography will make or break how your work looks.

Storage Space

Another area important to your business is the storage space needed for your samples. Among the samples you will have to inventory are fabric for draperies and upholstery, hard window treatments and blinds, shutters, wallpaper, carpet and other flooring, bedding, and paint, just to name a few. If your office is large enough, you can set up your samples on a wall with one of the various sample rack systems available. One of the easiest and least expensive ways to do so is with pegboard. Panel your wall with it, leaving enough space between the pegboard and wall to use S-hooks to hang your samples. Combine this system with a few shelves and you will be able to fit a large amount of samples in a small space. Some of your sales representatives will try to sell you the costly racks that have been designed for their samples, but unless you are in a showroom setting, they are not worth the money. Remember, no one will see them but you.

Off-Site Storage Space

You will also need a space for incoming products and deliveries. Some of the products, such as long blinds or carpet rolls, or sofas, can be quite large and require a lot of storage space. These are not items you wish to have come to your home and most vendors will not deliver to a private residence. The solution is to contract with a local freight company and warehouse. Arrange to have your products and furnishings sent there and for them to make the local delivery or your installer may be able to pick up there. There are storage and receiving fees, but it's a part of doing business. Negotiate to pay monthly—this is the most convenient method.

Your garage or storage shed will serve your purposes for the rest of your deliveries. Make sure that your storage space will stay dry in bad weather, because you will be receiving fabrics and other delicate goods. You will also have UPS and other delivery companies knocking at your door daily. Build a rapport with the drivers, so that they will leave the delivery in the appropriate place and not out in the rain or snow when you're not at home. You should have a business insurance policy in place that will cover losses of merchandise stored at your house or in your car.

Use a Bonded Warehouse

Be sure the warehouse you choose to accept your carpet or furniture is insured against damage after it is received by the warehouse. You may need to leave some products longer than usual due to a delay in construction—be safe!

Your Car

You will have a second office while operating your new business—your car. Between running to and from appointments and marketing your business, most of your time will be spent in your office-away-from-your-office. A minivan is used frequently in this business because it's easy to keep your samples and paperwork organized. Of course, when starting out, you should work with what you have until you absolutely need the upgrade. Your car or van needs to be in good working order and clean and sparkling to make the best impression.

You will carry with you the samples that you tend to use the most, along with the price lists that go with them. This will eliminate the need to lug them to and from your office daily. Business cards, a tape measure, a portable calculator, invoices, and a notebook will also be carried in your car.

It's hard to keep your car efficient and organized without a system. Set up boxes in the trunk and put the samples in them, arranging them according to the frequency of use. Another box in the backseat can hold the price lists, invoices, and other paperwork. In addition, your briefcase that you carry with you at all times should hold your business cards, pens, calculator, tape measure, and duplicates of any forms you might need.

It sounds like a lot of preplanning and backup, but it's necessary to appear professional. Designers frequently win bids from competitors whose clients lost faith in them because they were messy and unorganized. Always present yourself as a professional and you will be that much ahead of your competition.

A Word about Your Appearance

There are two schools of thought on the subject of appearance. One says that if you own your own business you can dress however you want, the assumption being that if you like casual clothes, they should work just fine. But your clients may wonder how you will put their homes together if you can't put yourself together with a pleasing, professional appearance. We're in the business of style, so how we present our professional selves needs to reflect our professional standing. Leave the casual-comfies for days when you are working from home and have no appointments—probably the best part of working from home!

How you dress should appeal to your target clientele and be appropriate for the tasks you will be performing. An interior design consultant will likely be more "dressed up" than someone who is running up and down ladders. You will look just as unprofessional in a short skirt and heels climbing a ladder or on your knees measuring a floor as your colleagues in old jeans and sweatshirts.

The trick is to put together a professional wardrobe that's flexible, and it doesn't have to break your budget. Look through your closet: You'd be surprised at what pieces you might find look perfect when paired with a new item. Don't assume a professional look has to be boring, either, especially for someone whose job needs to reflect his or her creative flair.

Pair a hot new color with a simple black skirt. By adding a great color, you show off your color sense. If you're a suit person, pair it with unusual scarves or that funky little pin you found on your last vacation. Unusual colors work for men, too. Pair those slacks with a new shirt in the latest fashion color. Pick a tie with an intriguing design. Wear a suit or jacket and slacks for meetings or big appointments, and add a little flair with a tie, or maybe a pair of unusual socks.

Good grooming, hair and nails all should be part of your regular routine.

The main point is: Look the part of a professional, but always let your personality shine through.

Defining Your Business

You need to decide how you want to set up your business legally. Your four main choices are sole proprietorship, partnership, limited liability company (LLC), or corporation. There are pluses and minuses to all three types of businesses. This section touches on the basics, but you will need to contact a lawyer or accountant and discuss your options.

Sole Proprietorship

This is the easiest type of business to start with because it's just you and no one else. The upside is that it's a quick and easy set-up; however, there can be big downsides. In this business structure, your personal and business finances are not separate and there is no protection for your personal assets should something happen in your business. If you default on a loan or if you become ill and a client sues you for not fulfilling an order, your personal assets are at risk. Additionally, it can be much harder to obtain a business loan under this structure.

Partnership

In a partnership, two or more people share the ownership of a single business. This includes all assets, financial contributions, decision making, and profit sharing.

This type of business can be tricky. Many people go into business with a friend, acquaintance, or family member and experience a huge success. On the other hand, many friendships have been severed and family relationships soured because the partnership went bad. If you are thinking of going into business with someone, make sure you are compatible in every way.

When starting this type of business, a partnership agreement is mandatory. This agreement is prepared by an attorney, and it can be costly. It will outline every aspect of your business and answer tricky questions on the chance that they arise. For instance, imagine that you went into business with your best friend. You are the outgoing designer who prefers to work with residential clients, while your partner is a business-minded designer who thrives in the corporate atmosphere. It sounds like the perfect match, so you skip the partnership agreement. After all, if you can't trust your best friend, whom can you trust? Everything goes fine for the first four years, the business is turning a profit, and both of you are living quite comfortably. You are acquiring a large share of the marketplace and your competitors are getting nervous. One of them makes you an offer to buy your business at a substantial profit. You want to jump at the chance—it would mean a lot of upfront cash in your pocket—but your business-minded partner sees the potential of the business and is willing to spend the next five or ten years building it up before even considering a sale. The two of you are at a standstill, each firmly believing you are right.

The partnership is in jeopardy and there is no legal backup. If you had a partnership agreement, there would not be a problem. The partnership agreement would have answered that question before it arose, everything would have been worked out beforehand, and there would be no surprises.

Another way to safeguard your business is to invest in partnership insurance, which covers you against any lawsuits arising from your partner's actions.

Try to find a partner who has the skills that you lack. If you are great in marketing for new customers but lack management skills, be sure your partner is management material. One benefit to having a partner is that your partner will be contributing to the finances of the company in addition to drawing from the profits. Another advantage is that you will not be entirely responsible for everything. If you get that headache, there will be someone to deal with the irate customer. The key to the success of the partnership is finding the right partner—not an easy task.

The downside to a partnership is similar to a sole-proprietorship, where you both are personally liable for any business expenses or damages that may arise. There are also additional tax obligations in a partnership. A good tax attorney or accountant will help you navigate these waters.

Limited Liability Company

An LLC is a kind of hybrid between a partnership structure and a corporation. As with corporations, there are limits to your personal liability and as with a partnership there are tax efficiencies and more operational flexibility. Owners are called *members* and there can be one or more owners. There is no separate income tax reporting for the business and profits and losses are passed through to the individual members to be reported on their personal tax returns. The downside to an LLC is that it has a limited life-span and if one member leaves the company, the LLC is dissolved and has to be restructured to move forward.

Corporation

A corporation (aka *C corporation*) is an independent legal entity that is owned by its shareholders. There is a clear wall separating your personal financial assets from the business and this format offers a great deal of protection. Unlike many small businesses, interior design industry liabilities can be substantial. Even if you're only doing a modest amount of business, your ongoing accounts could easily total $30,000 at any given time. In a corporation, unlike a sole proprietorship, the corporation is responsible for any debts incurred; you personally are not liable. Your tax structure will be different if you decide to incorporate. You will probably need to hire a certified public accountant to explain the ins and outs of the corporate tax laws. Generally speaking, though, the amount of cost to set up and run the corporation doesn't make a lot of sense for a single-person entity with no employees. There are other ways to protect your assets.

Existing Businesses and Franchises

You have the option of buying a design firm that has been in business for a while or buying a franchise, which is the name and operation procedures of a known existing company. Let's discuss each of these.

Existing Companies

You may have seen advertisements for an interior design business that is for sale. "Wouldn't it be easier for me to buy one that is already up and running?" you ask. Probably not. This business is commonly referred to as a "blue sky" business, meaning that there are no assets, equipment, or tools that have any real-world value. The biggest asset in this type of company is you, the designer, and the relationship you have built with the community. Customer satisfaction is the key to a successful interior design business. There is no way of knowing a previously owned-and-operated business's true reputation in the marketplace.

Another reason not to go this route is the money: While it is relatively inexpensive to purchase this type of business, all you are getting is the name, which you can't be sure is any good. An exception to this rule is if you have worked for this firm and know the value of its current clients and further growth.

Franchises

There are some well-established interior design franchises on the market and buying into an already established company may seem like a great quick-start plan. However, the start-up costs are very high, and after you have paid the initial fee, you will have to continue to pay the franchiser a portion of your retail sales for the life of your business. You will not (usually) be allowed to choose your own vendors in a franchise and you will likely have to work in the design style that the franchise is known for. Ultimately, you can start your own business for much less money, and you will truly be your own boss.

Your Business Name

Now that your office space is set up and you have decided on the legalities, it's time to name your business. The name you choose for your business is important because it portrays an image to the public, and you want to be sure it's the right one. Changing your business name can be time consuming and costly, as well as confusing in the marketplace, so think carefully before you commit.

There are many considerations when choosing a name for your business. You can select a name that really spells it all out like "Dependable Window Coverings and Design." A name like this will likely appeal to a wide market of new homeowners and people wanting to remodel their homes. They will probably be in the market for window coverings as well as other products and design services. They will also probably be looking for a budget price and if that's the market you're going for, the clarity of the business name will serve you well.

Let's say you decide to name your business "New Wave Design." Some people may understand that you are an interior design business, but others may think you are a hair studio. Let's change that and call the business "New Wave Interiors." Now that the name is clear, what kind of message does it send? Most people who call New Wave Interiors would probably be interested in hiring a designer with a contemporary style. It might be hard to reach customers with product-only needs or those whose tastes are more traditional. In the end, your company name should reflect the focus of your business. If you are offering design consulting services then using your own name—"[Your Name] Interior Design"—or New Wave Interiors will speak to your overall design focus. If your business is more product driven, you will want to highlight that focus in your business name. In subsequent chapters, we'll use "Dependable Window Coverings and Design" in examples of forms and procedures.

The Paper Trail

The state and federal governments require a great deal of paperwork from small business owners. Monthly or quarterly tax filings are required. Follow the rules, be on time with tax payments, and your business should run smoothly.

Assumed Name or Fictitious Name Certificate

You will fill out an assumed name or fictitious name certificate form at your local county courthouse or town hall, declaring your intention to go into business. This form registers the name you have chosen for your business. Each locality has different rules for setting up a business, even a home-based business, so check your local laws. You will need a certified copy of this document to set up your business bank account.

Tax Resale Number

In most states you have to charge taxes on any goods that you sell. You are, in essence, an agent for the state, and as such, it's your job to collect the tax owed and pass it along to the state in the form of monthly or quarterly payments. Simply go to your local tax collector's office and apply for a number; most applications can be made online. The tax rate varies in all states, and your local representative will explain the one that applies to you. Be very careful to pay everything that is due, and pay it on time. Consider setting up a separate bank account just for the sales tax you collect; this is one way to ensure that funds do not accidentally become crossed or that you're not short for the amount due. You also need this certificate to set up wholesale and trade-only industry accounts.

Federal ID Number

You will need this if you hire full-time employees in your business; if you don't have employees your social security number will double as your federal ID. When it comes time to hire a regular employee, contact your local officials to request a number.

Contractor Licenses

Some states require licenses for contractors doing specific jobs. Check with your local authorities to determine what you need a license for and what requirements need to be met.

Business Bank Account

You will need a separate bank account for your business. Most manufacturers will not set up a wholesale account with you unless there is a bank account designated for your business. Your bank will advise you on what documents they require, but it's likely to be your assumed name certificate and resale number.

Insurance

According to the Independent Insurance Agents of America, more than one half of home-based businesses aren't sufficiently insured. The biggest mistake business owners make is believing that they are covered under their homeowners policy, but in reality a typical homeowners policy will only insure a very limited amount of business items in your home and will not cover items that are taken out of the home (i.e., when you are on appointments).

Since each business situation is different, you will need to do some research and determine exactly what your needs are. Use the checklist in this section when thinking about your specific needs. Then talk to your insurance agent and determine which of the following policies are right for you and your business.

- **Property insurance.** This policy covers your business equipment, furnishings, and samples.

- **Business property insurance.** This covers business equipment taken out of the home, like credit-card machines, laptop computers, and installation tools.

- **Health insurance.** Historically difficult to obtain as an individual, the new insurance exchanges at the state or federal level will allow you to sign up for coverage as an individual.

- **Professional liability insurance.** Also known as *errors and omissions insurance*, professional liability insurance offers protection for your professional advice or the failure of a product you sell a client to perform. In medicine this is called *malpractice insurance*.

- **Business interruption insurance.** This policy protects against natural disasters, such as a fire or flood that would keep you from operating your business.

- **Life insurance.** This is especially important if you are the head of household. Your family depends on you to provide for them.

- **Workers' compensation insurance.** The laws vary in each state, so when you hire employees, check to find out what is required.

- **Auto insurance.** Check with your insurance agent to find out what provisions you must add to be insured in the event of an accident while working.

- **Bonds.** Most of your professional workers will be bonded. A carpet layer or other full-time contractor is required in most states to post bond. This means that if you hire a carpet layer and the person messes up the installation or there is other damage or theft, you (and your client) will be protected by the bond. In some cases when working with builders or on commercial jobs, the contract will require that your company be bonded. This gives them the same protection if you somehow mess up the job or are unable to complete it. It is possible in some instances to ask the builder or commercial contact to temporarily add you to their policy. If they won't, check with your insurance agent because the price and guidelines of each policy will depend on the job.

- **General Liability Insurance.** If you are measuring the windows in a client's home and accidentally break a 2,000-year-old vase, who pays for it? Your insurance company, if you carry liability insurance. It's wise to carry liability insurance on your business for many reasons. A client could sue you if he or she simply trips on a phone cord in your office and gets hurt. Again, your liability insurance should cover any injuries or damages sustained. Your insurance agent will outline the costs, deductibles, and rules of this particular type of policy.

- **Disability Insurance.** This insurance is especially important if you are running a sole proprietorship, and it is one of the most overlooked policies. With this policy, if you are forced to be out of work because of an accident or something else out of your control, a portion of your salary will be paid by the insurance company for a predetermined period of time. There are many variations to this type of policy. Research your alternatives in depth before making any decisions.

Remember to do your research before you choose an agent. Talk to a few companies. Appendix A has some additional resources on the topic of insurance.

Insurance Question Checklist

- Total amount of business equipment (e.g., samples, computer)
- Will you carry inventory? If so, how much? (Reduced-priced fabric or carpet rolls?)
- What will it cost to run your business every month? (disability)
- Will you be working with builders? (bonds, workers' compensation)

- What if you broke an antique vase in your customer's home while measuring a window? (business liability)

Insurance Tip Sheet

- Review your policy annually as your business grows.

- Shop around for the best rate but don't skimp on coverage.

- Try to work with only one agent. Let him or her get to know your business.

- Insist that your contractors carry their own insurance—it will greatly reduce your costs.

- Keep a copy of your installers' policies in your file and update annually. You will be asked to furnish proof of coverage.

What Is This Going to Cost?

Clearly, setting up shop requires a lot of important research. You also need cost estimates to determine your start-up costs, which we'll focus on in chapter 3.

03 | Start-Up Costs

The next step in setting up your business is to determine what your start-up costs will be. When first starting out in business, you should keep your costs to a minimum, investing only in the necessities. Later, when your business is making a profit, you can add the luxuries if you so desire. In this chapter we will explore the various purchases you will need to make and complete a personalized start-up cost worksheet using the information from the research you conducted in the previous chapter. The worksheet will give you an idea of how much it will cost to open the doors of your new business. This chapter can be complex, but it is vital to the success of your business, so don't skip over it.

What It Will Cost to Start Your Business

The start-up costs that you need to consider are basic office supplies, a computer and necessary software, samples, advertising, licenses, insurance, telephone, working capital, personal reserve, and any remodeling you may do in setting up your office space. It is impossible to provide you with the exact figures of these items because each case will be different. Do some research to determine what the charges are in your area for each of the items listed. Then plug those figures into the start-up cost worksheet later in this chapter and you will get a reliable picture of the amount of money needed to start your business. This figure will be the basis of your business plan that is discussed in chapter 4. If you have some cash put away and do not plan on applying for a loan, it is still essential that you have a good business plan. Without one, you won't have a good idea where your business is headed, or even if it is going in the right direction. A business trying to make it without a business plan is like a train trying to run without tracks.

Doing the Books

To run a successful interior design business, you must be good at design and have a business mind. If you have any doubts, hire someone to do your books for you, but never give up oversight and control over what's happening with your financials. It will be an additional expense, and one that you probably don't need when you're just starting out, but it may save your business in the long run. Even if you don't think you're "good with numbers" you can learn how to read a profit and loss statement and pay attention to your cash flow. Call around to determine the costs in your area, which can run from $50 to $100 an hour. A good bookkeeper will help you get your books set up appropriately for your business model, but ongoing work may not take too many hours a month to keep up with.

If you plan on doing your own bookkeeping, there are good software programs on the market that will make it easier. Do your research to determine which is best suited to your needs. The most commonly used program for small business is Quickbooks. More are listed in appendix A.

Your research will guide you in filling out the start-up cost worksheet, except for a few areas. Your initial advertising will vary depending on where you live and how much you plan on advertising. Be sure to read chapter 6 before filling in that blank. You also should plan on having three months of working capital and personal capital in the bank before you start your business.

You already know how much it costs you to live (add your personal expenses of mortgage or rent, car payments, food purchases, electric and phone bills, any loan or credit card payments, and miscellaneous expenses). Use the general overhead section of the profit-and-loss worksheet in chapter 5 as a guide to arrive at this number.

Buying and Using a Computer

Before you jump right in and purchase a computer, there are a few things to consider.

Type

Do you want to use a laptop or desktop computer? What about a tablet? You will have to determine which will best suit your needs. Laptops and tablets are great and offer a wealth of information at your fingertips at all times. There is Wi-Fi almost everywhere, and it is always nice to have access to price lists and formulas while on the road. A desktop has the advantage of a larger screen, which is very helpful with any computer-aided design (CAD) programs you may be working with or even if you're just toggling back and forth between different spreadsheets while

Start-Up Cost Worksheet

Fixtures and equipment (samples, camera, computer, car, etc.)	$_____
Remodeling costs for new office	$_____
Office supplies	$_____
Business cards and stationery	$_____
Licenses and permits	$_____
Legal and bookkeeping fees	$_____
Insurance	$_____
Telephone and internet	$_____
Initial advertising	$_____
Working capital (3 months)	$_____
Personal expenses (3 months)	$_____
TOTAL	$_____

working up an estimate. Tablets and smart phones come with lots of great apps (applications), plus a pretty decent everyday camera. Many vendors and service providers are offering easy app access to their information, which can be very useful. Another factor on a computer purchase is to determine what your software needs will be. If you're doing closet design, there will be a software package that will have specific hardware requirements, as do CAD programs and contact management software. It's a big purchase, so take the time to carefully consider your needs. If you have a dedicated computer, do what you can to make it work as long as possible. Do not use a shared family computer and keep your computer off limits to family. You want it in good working order at all times, with no surprise viruses that were accidentally downloaded, and always available when you need it. A dedicated computer and all associated peripherals such as printers and cameras are tax-deductible business expenses as long as they are being used solely for business purposes.

Internet Access

For all the uses mentioned previously, it's absolutely vital to have reliable, high-speed internet access. One of the downsides of working from home is that we might not appear as "professional" as someone with a store front or office. This can result in lost business or at the least customers who think we shouldn't charge as much as the guy with the store down the street. We need to make sure by all outer appearances, we have a professional operation.

Make the Internet Work for You

- Widen your search options when client shopping to worldwide resources.

- Check on current availability of a product.

- Join online trade groups for peer support and inspiration.

- Stay up to date on current trends in colors, fabrics, and furnishings.

- Market your services and products to a wider audience. E-design (aka *long distance design*) is common and products can always be shipped.

Your Website

It is absolutely necessary for anyone in business today to have a website. Since so few people use the Yellow Pages, the only way you will be found, outside of personal referrals, networking, and paid advertising, is through your own web marketing initiatives. The kind of site you have and how it's set up depends on your business focus. Most consulting interior designers have what used to be called a "business card site" and is now more appropriately called a "portfolio site." If you are primarily selling product, you can either have a website that showcases your wares, the product lines, examples of installations, and so on, or you could move into a full-on e-commerce site where you are selling products direct to consumers via your online store.

Portfolio Site (aka *Business Card Site*)

If you need to establish a presence on the internet, but you aren't selling product, then a portfolio site is the site for you. Your website should tell the Who, What, Where, When, and Why of your business and showcase your work. (There's more about this in chapter 6.) Any time your business is mentioned, in an advertisement for example, your website should be listed. It gives you the opportunity to "flesh out" your business in exactly the manner you want to. Some designers report that their website is their main source of new client calls as the vast majority of those looking for resources are doing internet searches.

E-Commerce Site

If you are planning for Internet sales to make up a portion of your yearly sales, then you'll need a website that allows consumers to purchase those products online. To accomplish this process, your site will have to contain a catalog of your products, a shopping cart, and the ability to accept credit cards. Before setting up a website, be sure to visit the web and do some serious research to determine the competition and pricing structures in each category. There is a lot of competition in this space and many large companies are doing it very well. For a small business, the personal touch is usually your best feature.

The Basics of Website Development

It is possible to construct a website yourself by using one of the various software packages available on today's market. But if you're not technologically minded, you might have to hire a professional to do it for you. Plan to spend a few hundred dollars for the software if you're going to build the site yourself. Hiring a web designer will usually start around $1,500 for a portfolio site that has multiple pages. The more bells and whistles you include, the bigger the bill will be. If you absolutely cannot swing that kind of price tag, then at least get a great looking one-page website up that has a representative photo of your work, a little about what makes you unique and your contact information. You can always expand later on as funds become available.

Websites require hosting services (Network Solutions or GoDaddy to name two large ones) and there are monthly or annual fees for this service. If you're hiring a website designer, they will be able to advise you on this subject. Plan to pay an Internet service provider at least $200 per year for hosting services. Try to find a host that offers free e-mail so that your e-mail address will match your website address (and be more memorable).

Finally, you will have to advertise your website, just as you will your off-line business. Look for information about Internet advertising in chapter 6.

Samples

Samples are the lifeblood of your business. Without them you could not sell your product and services. Each manufacturer produces books of samples that represent its various products in a designer fashion. You will use these samples to aid the expression of your ideas.

You should be able to fill in all of the blanks on the start-up cost worksheet except for the one titled "Fixtures and Equipment." Included in this item are samples, and I will discuss them now. There is a sample book for every product that you sell. These include carpet binders, fabric books, paint wheels, and window covering sample books. Because you will be working out of your home, you will not be able to rely on the large vignettes and product displays that the larger stores do. (You won't have their high overhead, either!) Instead, you will carry with you samples of all the products that you sell.

There are quite a few manufacturers or vendors for each product. See appendix A for a list of many popular vendors sorted by product type. Each manufacturer will be represented by a salesperson called a *manufacturer's representative*. As a business owner, you will have to decide what companies you want to work with and what product best suits your and your client's needs. Some product types are represented by several different manufacturers. Pricing and service will be the deciding factors in choosing your suppliers. Consulting interior designers may have direct trade accounts with manufacturers for fabrics, lighting, or furnishings, or they may work through a local design center that stocks samples of their product lines for the designer to borrow or bring clients to see.

Sample Books

The prices of sample books vary. Take for instance the window covering samples. The books can run about $250 from some manufacturers, but another one may decide to give them to you for free. Most of the time it is left up to the sales representative to determine the distribution of the company's books. If you can convince sales representatives that you will sell a great amount of their product, they will be more likely to give you the books for free. Of course, that may be hard to do when just starting out in business. This is another argument in favor of working for someone else first. Not only will you get the experience you need, you will also get to know the sales representatives and increase your chances of not having to pay for their samples. You may have to pay for some upfront sample books, but over time as your sales increase, they will be more likely to give you one for free every now and then. Smaller manufacturers are usually more liberal with their samples.

Some manufacturers offer a sample rebate program. If you purchase a certain amount of goods as your first purchase or within a set period of time, they rebate you the price of the book. This is not only a good way to save money on sample books, it's also very motivational!

One obstacle you may run into when purchasing samples is the "sample plan." Some manufacturers insist that if you do business with them, you must purchase sight unseen preselected samples from them every month or so. Wallpaper and the larger fabric companies usually operate this way. The idea behind the plan is that you own a showroom and have plenty of room to stock their samples. These sample plans vary in cost, but they can run anywhere from $200 to $1,500 per month. Obviously, it is not prudent for a home-based designer to work with these programs, but don't worry—there are other options. The most obvious is to not do business with these manufacturers. There are an abundant number of suppliers out there who are willing to sell to you on less stringent terms. The problem is that most of the companies that use sample plans are well known in the consumer marketplace. Because of this, some of your customers may request that you use a particular brand on their job. You don't want to have to outlay that kind of money on the off chance that one of your customers will request one of these products. On the other hand, you want to be able to accommodate their needs. Enter designer showrooms.

Designer Showrooms

A designer showroom is a privately owned business that sells products to designers at discounted prices, also called *net pricing*. The showroom will generally carry a large selection of drapery fabrics, upholstery fabrics, wallpaper, carpet, flooring, ceramic tile, hard window coverings, paint, lighting, furniture, and accessories. Great, you say, why even bother to purchase my own samples? In some cases it doesn't make any sense to stock your own samples simply because you can't stock as much as a showroom can. On the other hand, you are giving up some of your profit because you are one step removed from the manufacturer. To retain your same profit, you would need to pass this additional markup directly to your customer, which you may not wish to do.

Rather than selling you the product at a wholesale rate, showrooms are adding their profit margin onto their buying price and calling it the "net" designer price. That means if you are doing a carpet job and would normally buy a piece of carpet for $2,000 from a manufacturer, you might have to pay up to $2,600 for it at a showroom. If you're bidding out jobs and they are done on a competitive basis, the $600 will likely come out of your pocket, not your client's. That means if you were planning on selling the job for $4,000 and making a $2,000 profit, you are now down to a $1,400 profit. The smart choice is to open direct accounts with the vendors you feel that you like the most and will have the most market appeal, but use the designer showrooms to expand upon your offerings and keep your designs fresh and unique from project to project.

The sample comparative chart in this chapter can help you determine which manufacturer is giving you the best deal on samples. Gather all the information on each company you are considering by type (carpet, fabric, shutters, etc.) and fill out a chart for each type of product. All other things being equal, you will want to go with the manufacturer who is offering you the best deal—pricing on the product itself and the cost of their samples.

Writing Your Business Plan

Think of a business plan as a road map. You wouldn't drive a car across the country without a road map (or GPS), would you? You shouldn't start a business without one either. It may be possible to run a business without a plan, but you will put yourself at an immediate disadvantage. Many people go into business, especially interior design, because they are enamored with the idea that interior design and entrepreneurship are glamorous and exciting. And it can be, but it's a business first and foremost and setting up and running a good business should be your primary concern. The freedom and glamour will come, but only when it's resting on the foundation of a good business structure.

One of the primary purposes of a business plan is to attract startup funding. If you are going to present it to a bank or another lender for start-up capital, you will need to focus on the hows and whens of repayment. It is rare that a new home-based business will qualify for a traditional business loan, however. More likely, you are self-funding your venture, or possibly borrowing money from family. Even so, you should write your plan and operate your business in the same manner. If you've borrowed your startup capital from family, you will want to set up a repayment plan. Just as importantly, if you're taking cash from your own savings, you should consider it a loan from yourself, or your household, that also needs to be paid back by a predetermined date. Your business plan will help focus your attention on the business of your business and keep you on track for achieving success.

A business plan is broken down into several main sections:

- The Executive Summary
- Company Profile
- Products and Services
- Market Analysis

- Marketing and Sales

- Finances

This chapter will guide you step by step through the overall process of writing your business plan and make it as straightforward as possible. There are many books and online resources available that will really help you delve into the finer points of a business plan. Your own accountant is also a great resource for putting together your financial information.

The Executive Summary

This is a brief summary of your entire business and business plan. As such, you should wait until you've written all the other sections and then circle back to write your executive summary. As a new business, your summary will be focused on why you are opening your business and how your experience and background will lead to the success of the new venture. You will briefly discuss your market analysis and any needs or gaps in your market that you are seeking to fill and how you intend to fill it. If you are seeking third-party funding, this is the place where you will convince potential funders that you are a worthy risk. If you're not seeking outside funding, this is the place you might come to give yourself a little boost of encouragement.

Company Profile

You could hire a motivation expert or business consultant to help you define your business's vision and direction, also known as a *mission statement,* but nobody knows better than you how you want to shape your company's image. A mission statement is a brief sentence or two summarizing your purpose and goals for your business. Here is an example of one written with the aid of an expert, at a cost of $750:

> *Our goal is to design our customers' homes with a sense of style that is unique. We will always keep humor as a constant in our work attitude. Our customers' satisfaction is the ultimate goal.*

While it seems simple, it takes some real work to boil down all your thoughts and ideas into something so brief. As you write, just concentrate on what will make your business unique in the marketplace. Sure, you want to design homes, but how? Will you concentrate on one style of design or have an eclectic style? Will you work with wealthy clients or concentrate on middle-income families? Will you put customer satisfaction above everything else? (If you said no to this question, please refer to chapter 1.) You should be able to answer all these questions with your mission statement.

Providing Your General Business Description

In the general business description, you should detail the basics of your business.

Start with your business name, the legal setup of your business (sole proprietorship, partnership, or corporation), the name of the owner or partners, the main source of income (residential or commercial), the business address, and your background and education in your field of endeavor.

You will be providing a more full business description about the nature of your business and the products and services you will be offering. In the upcoming sections on Products and Services and Market Analysis you will be going into further depth, but your general business description should include a few sentences about these areas as well. Here are a couple of examples:

> *Dependable Window Coverings and Design will be providing quality window and wall coverings as well as flooring for a residential clientele that is design oriented and price conscious. Our goal is to bring both function and beauty to our clients' homes with excellent products in a range of prices while also providing interior design services as needed. Our differentiating factor in the marketplace is that we are able to offer design advice along with carrying a wide array of attractive products.*

or

> *New Wave Interiors offers a broad range of interior design consulting services from color consultations to window treatment design through whole-room and home-design planning. Our customers will be design-savvy professionals who are looking for beauty and quality, and enjoy being a part of the design process. In addition to design consulting, we will be offering access to exclusive trade-only goods and furnishings as well as custom-made items using only the best workrooms. Our differentiating factor in the marketplace is that we are client focused and bring a deep knowledge of products and technology to the process.*

In both cases, we have shared our primary business focus—products or design consulting—and that we have knowledge beyond that primary focus. We're establishing who our clients will be and our differentiating factors in the marketplace.

Products and Services

Defining Your Business

You will use the section that defines your business to sell your business ideas to a potential lender. When writing this section, imagine how you'll be viewed by the person lending the money. What will you offer to the public that will make people want to do business with you? Do you have any experience in the field? Are you an accomplished salesperson? Do you have an uncanny knack for putting colors together? If so, state it. To many people, interior design is basically fluff and not a necessity. This is the place to make a case for why this is not so. You might discuss the functional nature of window treatments (lighting and heat control) or how through your services, your clients are less likely to make costly mistakes such as ordering the wrong size furniture or bringing in subpar installers. Make a list of the products and services you plan to offer. Your list might look something like the one that follows.

You also will need to include in this section of your plan what your intended charges are for your products and services. Chapter 7 discusses how to set your prices. This is the place where you will include your research on your competition and how you intend to compete with more established businesses. A lender will feel more confident in you if you've done the market research and are knowledgeable in the field. In addition, knowing what market you are trying to penetrate can only increase your chances of success. Provide a list of your estimated charges for each of the products. Since it will be impossible to list each price separately, you might show a range of high and low prices for each of the major products you will be selling. For example, window shades will range from $1,500 to $250 per window or decorator fabric ranges from $200 per yard to $40 per yard. As for your design consultation fees, shop around and find out what your competition is charging. Most beginning designers charge between $50 and $75 per hour, but it's really based on what the market will bear. In this field, the low price is not necessarily the best. Be careful of "lowballing" (selling the product or service at a substantially lower price than the market demands). Lenders will be wary of this tactic because these types of businesses don't tend to stay in business for very long.

Market Analysis

As part of contemplating a new business, you must know if there is a market for your products and services. It's a mistake to assume that anyone that lives in a

Products Offered

- Hardline window treatments including blinds, shutters, cellular shades
- Soft treatments including drapery, valances, shades, cornice boards, bedding, pillows, and cushions
- Flooring products including carpet, tile, wood, and vinyl
- Wallpaper
- Designer fabrics for drapery and upholstery

Services Offered

- Interior design consultation services including color consultations, finishes and fixtures, window treatment and upholstered furniture design, floor plans, whole-room and whole-house decorating
- Professional installation services for all products offered

home is a potential client or that all wealthy people are interested in spending a lot of money in their homes. Perhaps you're located in a high-tech town filled with young millionaires. It sounds good, but if you assume most are young men who are still living like college students (bank accounts notwithstanding), they may not be a ready client base.

Your market analysis should include the demographics of your target markets as well as their buying behaviors. Demographic information is fairly easy to find. Most towns publish their statistics based on regular community and national censuses. Buying behaviors are harder to come by but you can make some assumptions. For instance, are houses large or small? Are they well-tended with manicured lawns and luxury vehicles parked in the driveway? What kind of stores and other design services are available in the area? Finally, you may want to consider any seasonal changes that would affect your business. For instance, are you in a summer or winter destination that nearly shuts down in the off-season? If it's exclusive enough, your in-season business may make up for the slow season, but you need to understand this. The Small Business Administration offers a wealth of information about understanding your market.

You will also need to know who your competition is. This is generally as simple as driving around and seeing what stores and design businesses have brick and mortar shops, checking online for businesses with websites, and looking at member directories of local chambers of commerce and business networking groups. Make a list of each business, what they do and even how long they have been in business if that information is available. Are there a glut of similar businesses and how will you stand out from the crowd? Or are there very few design businesses? If so, does that mean there's a nice opening, or could it mean there are not enough clients to sustain a business? You might also do some research on how many allied businesses there are such as builders, architects, landscapers or realtors. The success of these businesses can be an indicator of how receptive the market is for an interior design business.

Finally, you will need to understand if there are any barriers or restrictions that might impede your plans. Do you need to be registered or certified in some way? What special requirements or zoning restrictions exist for a home-based business? In most cases, you will be able to work through these issues, so long as you know about them ahead of time.

Marketing and Sales

Devising Your Marketing Strategy

In chapter 6, we go into great detail about how to market and advertise your new business. In this part of your business plan, you will outline how you are going to go after your business through marketing and advertising. This section of the plan will let the lender know whether you have a realistic understanding of how to attract business. Again, even if you aren't planning on seeking funds from a lender, do this part anyway. Can you see so far how much it will help you in running your business?

You will want to include a list of the various marketing strategies you plan on incorporating, whom they will target, and their projected reach. You will also want to include a growth strategy, which might include personnel, training, equipment, and new product lines, or if you see your growth coming from many smaller clients or fewer larger clients who will continue to hire you over several years.

Beyond your marketing initiatives, you will also want to formulate a sales strategy. For instance, do you plan on being the only sales or design person with a back shop of administrative help? Or are you looking to bring on additional sales people or designers as part of the growth of your brand?

Perhaps you envision having a self-branded product line. How will your marketing and sales initiatives open up this avenue to you?

Finances

Forecasting Your Company Equipment and Setup

This is where the start-up costs worksheet that you have completed comes in handy. In this section you will be forecasting the equipment you will need over the next few years, including office furniture, computer equipment, automobiles, samples, and tools. If you plan on hiring another designer in three years, you must take into consideration the fact that you will need to add a computer and additional sample books, tools, and possibly even a larger storage space to handle the additional incoming product. Will you provide your new employee with an automobile, insurance, or paid holidays? All these considerations must be reflected in your figures.

Determining Your Organizational Setup

You know after reading the basic job description in chapter 1 that you will have many organizational duties. Once your business gets larger, you can think about hiring someone to take some of the load off you, but in the beginning, you're it. For this section give a brief description of what running your company will entail. Tell of plans to add employees as you see fit. You also might include in this section a list of your skills that will benefit the company. See the following example of a

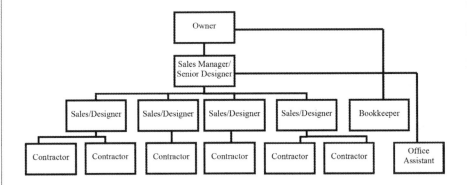

projected five-year employee plan.

Making Financial Projections

Doing the financial end of the business can be a challenge for new business owners. This section of the business plan will focus on your start-up and ongoing operations costs and estimating sales and revenue potential. If you have any doubts about being able to work out the numbers, your accountant will be able to help you.

Figuring Your Sales Potential

The interior design business is different from many other businesses because you will do any number of combinations of products and you may never do the same job twice. For instance, one client may require new carpet, some upholstery, and seven window shutters. That job may total $7,000. Your next job may only entail a color consultation for a new home. That job would probably run about $350. (These figures are to be used only as rough examples because prices vary in different parts of the country.) Let's assume an average sale of $1,000 per job and use that figure as an example for your forecasts. If you plan on working full time and are ambitious enough to aggressively market yourself, you might expect to do on average four jobs per month your first year in business. At $1,000 per job, your sales potential would be $4,000 per month. Note: these are gross sales figures not including cost of goods or other expenses. Remember also, these are average figures and as a new business, based out of the home, you can't necessarily expect as many as four new clients a month in the first several months or even the first year. This is your great "unknown" that makes financial projections so tricky.

Your next step is to turn your monthly projections into yearly projections. If you were able to generate an average of four jobs per month over the course of a year, your potential gross sales on these forty-eight jobs would be $48,000. Again, the operative word here is *potential*. On paper it doesn't look difficult, but the reality is much different. Now let's say the next year you manage to double the jobs that you do to eight per month but your per-job sale drops because each project is smaller, or you realize that you would rather work with fewer clients on larger projects and your yearly sales rise to $60,000 or $70,000. By the third year, you've got more business than you can handle, so you hire someone. Perhaps it will be an office assistant or bookkeeper, which opens up time in your schedule to do more marketing and take on more clients. Or your new employee might be a sales person or associate designer who is able to complete four or five jobs per month. Add that to your sales figures and you may be well into six figures. Do this month by month and then extend your figures to five years.

When you calculate your figures, be realistic and brutally honest with yourself about what kind of sales you really can generate, how much time you will have to invest in your business, and how much down time you will need. Do you live in an area that is depressed, or is the economy on an upswing? What do economists forecast for the next few years? Use these figures to guide you in your projections.

Sources for Start-Up Capital

Let's explore your options for financing your business. Following are ideas, ranging from the traditional to more alternative approaches.

- **Family and friends.** It's estimated that 85 percent of all new capital is borrowed from family and friends. This is the friendliest, easiest way to secure capital for your new business, and, after all, if you were going through a dry spell in your business, would your family really call the note due?

- **Banks.** This is the most often thought of way to finance a new business, but in reality less than 15 percent of new businesses go to a bank for a loan. And these days it's nearly impossible for a new business, especially a home-based operation with no track record, to secure financing. If you decide that it's best for you, be prepared with a strong business plan and proposal, and be ready to answer numerous questions regarding your business.

- **Credit cards.** Only use credit cards if your interest rate is fairly low and you are comfortable that you will be able to pay them back quickly. Misuse of credit cards can have disastrous results and weigh like an anchor around your neck.

Your financial statements should include prospective financial data projected out over the next five years. Even though you haven't begun operations yet, it's important to take all your known information (your startup costs from chapter 3 for instance) and make projections (also called *educated guesses*) where you have no hard data. Lenders would want to see forecasted income statements (as discussed previously), balance sheets, cash flow statements, and capital expense budgets. There are examples of balance sheets and cash flow statements in chapter 5. Your capital expense budgets are gleaned from your start-up costs and projected business growth estimates for major expenses such as computers and office equipment, company vehicles, and the like.

Finally, you should add as an appendix items that would support a request for financing such as your resume, awards and certificates, permits or licensing, and relevant magazine or news articles.

The interior design business is one of details. You have to be able to design with a sense of style as well as keep track of the books.

Keeping Track of Your Money

Accounting: Accrual or Cash Basis

The basic difference between the accrual system and the cash system is when income and expenses are recorded in your books. Generally, small businesses with under $5 million in billings will use the cash basis while larger or publicly traded companies use the accrual method.

With the accrual method, when you create an invoice and generate a receivable, it is recorded as collected money on the date of the invoice. Likewise, expense liabilities are generated when the item is delivered or service rendered, not when you pay for them. The accrual system doesn't work very well for interior design businesses because of the way money will be collected. When you accept a job, you will ask for a deposit against the total amount of the bill and collect the balance prior to delivery. If the turnaround is quick, say within a week, then accruing the balance due a week later, or simply collecting 100 percent up front, isn't that big of a deal. However, a sofa ordered in July can easily take eight to twelve weeks to arrive and with the accrual method your accounts will reflect the total sofa income in July rather than spread between July and October. While this method provides a more accurate snapshot of the overall health of your business, it doesn't capture your cash flow very easily as it's not related to your cash position. You could be showing excellent business returns on the books, but find out that there is no money in the bank.

The cash method records your income when you collect the money and deposit it into your bank. Similarly, expenses are accounted for when you pay a bill, not when you receive the good or service. Going back to the sofa referenced previously, let's say you sold a custom-designed sofa to your client for $8,000. You will be buying the fabric from the textile manufacturer ($1,400) and contract with a furniture workroom to build and upholster the sofa ($5,000), totaling $6,400 in your costs to produce the sofa. You mark up the sofa 25 percent for your profit for a total of $8,000. You write an invoice to the client for $8,000 (plus tax and delivery), and ask for a deposit of $4,875 upon order with the balance due prior to delivery. This $4,875 covers 100 percent of the cost of the fabric ($1,400), 50 percent for the workroom's required deposit ($2,500) and your 25 percent markup on these costs ($975). In October, you will owe the workroom the balance of their fee of $2,500 which you collect from your client (plus your remaining profit markup). Your books will better reflect your cash position with this method because all these separate transactions are recorded as they happened. (On a related note, many designers are now collecting 100 percent of the price of a piece of furniture rather than partial collections to protect themselves if the client changes their mind before the final payments are due.)

You will need a system to keep track of the dollars coming in and going out. A single-entry bookkeeping system is an easy method to keep track of your receivables and payables and may work during the early stages of a business before things really get up and running. On a daily basis simply enter any money you have collected from clients and then record any debits that you have made to your account. Then subtract the debits from the credits, and you should have a balance. In essence, a single entry system is much like your personal checkbook. A double-entry bookkeeping system is the one you ultimately should be using and is the standard for accountants, bookkeepers, and any accounting software you choose to use. As the name implies, when you enter a transaction into your accounting system, it is entered twice—once as a credit to one account and as a debit to another account. As transactions work their way from invoices to receivables or from bills to payables, there is always a check and balance going on to be sure you've entered your transactions properly. When you run a "balance sheet," it will come to zero (debits = credits) proving you're in balance. With this system you are able to run more in-depth reports to help you track your business. If in doubt, hire a bookkeeper or accountant to help you set up your system and keep it running smoothly.

Bookkeepers

A bookkeeper is someone who keeps track of your daily transactions (accounts receivable and accounts payable). For a small business the bookkeeper will generally come in once a week and enter all of the money that you've collected into

Balance worksheet as of _____ (Date) _____

For _____ (Name of business) _____

ACCOUNT	BALANCE
Assets	
Cash in bank/checking and savings	$_____
Petty cash	$_____
Other cash on hand	$_____
Accounts receivable	$_____
Office furniture and equipment	$_____
(Less depreciation)–	$_____
TOTAL ASSETS	$_____
Liabilities	
Accounts payable	$_____
Loans payable	$_____
Leases payable	$_____
Taxes	$_____
TOTAL LIABILITIES	$_____
Equity	
Current capital	$_____
Current net profit	$_____
(Less owner's salary)	$_____
TOTAL EQUITY	$_____
TOTAL LIABILITIES AND EQUITY	$_____

the accounts receivable column and write checks for any outstanding invoices you may have. Then the person will log those checks into your accounts payable column. Your bookkeeper doesn't need to be a signatory to your accounts and, unless the bookkeeper is a full-time employee, he or she should not have that access. The bookkeeper can write your checks for your signature, or if you pay bills online, he or she can set up the transaction but you hit the send button. This part of the bookkeeping is not hard; it just needs to be done in a consistent manner. It's easy to get behind and lose track of the status of your business and what direction it's headed. A good software program is essential to keeping things running smoothly.

Accountants

An accountant is probably the best value for your money. You should think of an accountant as your financial partner, someone able to give advice on various financial aspects of your business. For instance, if you have a good relationship with your accountant and you are considering expanding your business, he or she would be the best person to talk with about it. Your accountant has the ability to stand back and take a look at things from a purely financial aspect.

Your tax form will look a little different now that you own a business, and an accountant will be able to help you with that as well. They will complete the forms due at the end of the year as well as show you how to set up your business to reduce your tax debt. It is entirely possible to do your own books and run your own reports, but it's highly recommended that you hire an accountant to do your tax returns and to keep an eye on the overall health of your business, especially if you are thinking of incorporating.

Generating a Profit-and-Loss Statement

This report will tell you whether your business is making a profit or a loss. It can also serve a few other important purposes. As you have now discovered, you will be buying from many different manufacturers. One of the most important things the manufacturers will consider when assigning you a discount is the dollar amount of sales that you do with them. As your sales increase, so do your discounts. This report will not only help you keep track of the overall health of your business, it also will break down the dollar amount of business that you do with each supplier separately. Some companies will do this report once a month, others just once a year. You should be running a profit-and-loss statement once a month. If you have a computer program like Quickbooks, all you have to do is press a button and the report will be generated for you. (The program is tied into your bank records, so the

Accounting Records for the Week of (Date)

For _____ (Name of business)_____

Income_____

Date _____   SM _____   Amount $ _____

Date _____   SM _____   Amount $ _____

Date _____   SM _____   Amount $ _____

Date _____   SM _____   Amount $ _____

Date _____   SM _____   Amount $ _____

TOTAL INCOME $ _____

Expenses _____

Rent $ _____

Electricity $ _____

Phone $ _____

Debt payments $ _____

Salary $ _____

Commissions $ _____

Advertising payments $ _____

Manufacturer payments $ _____

Contract labor payments $ _____

Freight $ _____

TOTAL PAYMENTS $ _____

CURRENT BALANCE $ _____

information is simply formatted into the report.) An example of a typical profit-and-loss statement for an interior design business follows.

Begin the worksheet by entering in your total amount of sales as well as any other income that relates to your business. Next, you need to determine the amount of money that it costs you to sell the products. You will do this by entering the total amount of invoices you have for that period. You will notice that there are spaces for three different manufacturers after each category. You will use more than one manufacturer for each product, and by filling in the costs separately, you will be able to keep tabs on how much money you are spending with each vendor. Add the total amount of costs and subtract that from your gross sales; that will give you your total gross profit. Next, you will need to total your overhead expenses for the period of time that the profit-and-loss statement is to cover. Once you have that total, subtract it from your gross profit figure and you will finally arrive at your net profit total.

Making Cash Flow Projections

When operating a business, you will constantly have cash coming in and going out because you will be collecting checks from clients and paying vendors and bills. Your jobs and the sizes of them will also fluctuate and you will have to set aside money for quarterly and annual taxes and other big hits to your bottom line. Because of this you will need to keep constant tabs on your cash flow so that you don't get any nasty surprises. Use the following cash flow projections worksheet in your business consistently—weekly is best but should be no less than monthly—and it will help curtail hardship.

Accounts Receivable and Payable Files

You will need to keep track of money that is due in and bills that are to be paid out. This process doesn't have to be complicated. If you are using a software program this will be tracked for you and you can run regular reports to keep on top of your receivables and payables. If you are doing things "by hand" it's not terribly difficult but it does take some organization. You will need to set up files for accounts receivable, delinquent accounts, and accounts payable.

Accounts Receivable

Accounts receivable are the monies that are owed to you. In this business, the standard operating procedure is this: You should always collect your fees and product payments up front. If a client orders a sofa, they need to pay you a deposit upon placement of the order that is sufficient to cover your up-front costs, with the

PROFIT-AND-LOSS WORKSHEET FOR____ (Date) THROUGH_____(Date)_____

INCOME

Gross sales $_____

Other income $_____

TOTAL INCOME $_____

COST OF SALES EXPENSES
Blinds

Manufacturer #1 $_____

Manufacturer #2 $_____

Manufacturer #3 $_____

TOTAL BLINDS $_____

Fabric

Manufacturer #1 $_____

Manufacturer #2 $_____

Manufacturer #3 $_____

TOTAL FABRIC $_____

Flooring

Manufacturer #1 $_____

Manufacturer #2 $_____

Manufacturer #3 $_____

TOTAL FLOORING $_____

Labor

Manufacturer #1 $_____

Manufacturer #2 $_____

Manufacturer #3 $_____

TOTAL LABOR $_____

Wallpaper

Manufacturer #1 $_____

Manufacturer #2 $_____

Manufacturer #3 $_____

TOTAL WALLPAPER $_____

TOTAL COST OF SALES EXPENSES $_____

GROSS PROFIT $_____

(sales minus cost of sales expenses)

General overhead expenses

Accounts payable $_____

Advertising $_____

Automobile $_____

Cell phone $_____

Education $_____

Electric bill $_____

Freight $_____

Insurance $_____

Legal and professional fees $_____

Miscellaneous fees $_____

Office supplies $_____

Phone rental $_____

Referral fees $_____

Rent paid $_____

Samples $_____

Taxes $_____

Telephone $_____

Wages $_____

TOTAL GENERAL OVERHEAD EXPENSES $_____

NET PROFIT $_____

(gross profit minus total general overhead expenses)

Cash Flow Projections Worksheet

Month	Cash In Bank	Petty Cash	Collections	Total Cash	Expenses	Projected Expenses	Cash Balance
Jan.							
Feb.							
Mar.							
Apr.							
May							
June							
July							
Aug.							
Sept.							
Oct.							
Nov.							
Dec.							

balance due prior to delivery. Don't start the job without money in hand; promises are not sufficient. Most startups cannot withstand the negative cash-flow of paying for your clients' goods out of pocket and waiting for payment. When you create your invoice, you are creating a receivable that is either due upon receipt of invoice or is due prior to delivery of the product. You must have a method to help you keep track of this money. You're probably thinking right now that there's no way you're going to forget anyone who owes you money, but it's surprisingly easy. You may have many jobs going on at one time, or a few large jobs with many pieces and parts moving around creating myriad details to remember. You may not forget the $5,000 payment, but a $100 invoice will slip your mind faster than you might think. File the invoices alphabetically by the last name of your client (commonly referred to as the *sidemark [SM]*). Any invoices in this file reflect money that is owed to you either now or in the near future. When the invoice is paid, mark it as such and file it in the appropriate customer file. If you're running your account by hand, you will want to check this on a weekly basis and make sure everyone is current.

Delinquent Accounts

Hopefully you won't have any delinquent accounts, but even with the best of intentions, it can happen. Go through the accounts receivable file once a month and send out any delinquent notices that are necessary. If a customer becomes delinquent with an invoice, start taking steps to collect your money. If after numerous phone calls and letters from you, the customer still hasn't paid the bill, one option is to assign the debt to a collection agency. The figures vary, but the agency will take a percentage of the amount owed to you.

Another way to collect the debt is to file a lien against the property that you've worked on. Every state varies in its procedures, but as a general rule you as contractor have the right to place a lien on the property you've worked on within a certain number of days after the work is complete. (The amount of time varies, so check with your local authorities.) If you have to place a lien, it will sit on the records collecting interest until the homeowner sells the house or tries to refinance it. The title company will then search the records for any outstanding liens and pay them off with the proceeds of the sale. This is a drastic measure, but may be necessary if the project was large enough.

Accounts Payable

Accounts payable are the invoices that are owed by you to your vendors and contractors. It's entirely possible to have twenty or more invoices on the same job, so you'll need a system to keep track of them. The easiest way to do this is to use the same system that you use for your accounts receivable, but with another expandable file folder to file the invoices away after they've been paid. Your credit terms will be different with each of your vendors, so it's wise to look through this file weekly to avoid any late payments. Simply file each invoice under the name of the vendor. After you have paid the invoice, write paid and the date and the number of the check you used to pay it and file it in the accounts payable paid file. Any cash on delivery (COD) account invoices should go directly into the paid file. If you are negotiating better discounts with a vendor and want to prove how much business you have given that vendor over the last six months, simply pull invoices from the paid file and total them.

Ultimately, if you're planning on running a successful, professional business, you will need to be running a good accounting program that will manage all of this for you.

Change Orders

There will be times when you will be rolling through a job and the customer will change her or his mind about which carpet to use, or even about the trim color chosen for the bedspread. That's when a change order comes in. When you first accept a job, you will ask the customer to sign a contract that spells out the details and dollar amount of a job (more about this contract later in this chapter). As you make selections through the project, you should also be getting written sign-off on all decisions. If during the process, the client changes his or her mind, or perhaps a fabric ends up not being available, you should have the customer sign a change order, which is a form that spells out the exact changes as well as any dollar amount that changes. The importance of paying strict attention to the details of the contract and change orders can't be overstated. When a customer is doing a lot of work on his or her home, the details can get fuzzy. If a customer remembers that the draperies were supposed to be blue and they were made in pink, you would be in a tough position unless you had a contract or a change order with the customer's signature on it showing the selection or change. This chapter includes a sample change-order form that you can use in your business.

Customer Contracts

It is imperative to have all customers sign a contract before you begin work in their home. A contract serves to protect you and your customer from the inevitable discrepancies that occur when dealing with custom products. For example, let's imagine that you take an order from a client to install carpet in a room of her home. The color she's chosen is not in stock and has to be ordered from the mill.

Change Order

Date _____

Purchase Order Number _____

Customer Name _____

Address _____

Phone Number _____

Item to Be Changed _____

_____

_____

Difference in Price (+ or –) _____

I (the homeowner) agree that the above change items are true and requested by me. I will pay the difference in price if it is higher than the original invoice. I authorize the contractor to complete the changes as stated above.

CONTRACTOR_____   HOMEOWNER_____

You confirm the delivery date with the mill as two weeks from the order date. Your customer signs a contract and you order the carpet.

Because your business is new, the carpet mill requires a 50% deposit on the order to get it processed. You write the mill a check and sit back and wait. Two days before the order is due, the mill calls you to tell you the carpet has been delayed another two weeks. When the customer hears the news, she is so angry that she tells you to cancel the order. If you were to cancel the order, you would be out the 50% deposit that you sent the mill because that money is nonrefundable once the mill has started work on the order. Luckily, your client signed a contract, part of which states that you cannot be held responsible for acts of nature or manufacturing delays.

Credit Accounts for Your Business

Taking care of your personal and business credit is one of the most important things you can do for the growth of your business. If your personal credit rating isn't spotless, it will inhibit your business growth. One way you can help keep your credit in line is to stay on top of your record keeping. You will be overwhelmed with a daily barrage of paperwork. Be sure you know when your bills are due and pay them on time. Various methods can help you with the organization of your paperwork and so keep your credit report clear of blemishes.

When you buy from the various manufacturers, they will offer either an open account with credit terms or a pro forma account. Very little is done COD these days.

Open Accounts

When you operate with an open account, you will have a preestablished credit limit and a set amount of time to pay your invoices, which is usually 30 days. As a new business, it may be difficult to get an open account or the credit limit may be small at first. The benefit of an open account is twofold: it helps your cash flow in that you will have collected your client's payments before you have to pay the manufacturers' bills and you won't have to hold up orders waiting for your check to be received. Some manufacturers will offer you terms—an additional discount, typically 2 to 5 percent, for paying the invoice early. That means that if your invoice in the amount of $1,000 is due thirty days from the date of invoice, and you have terms of 2/10/net 30, you may deduct 2 percent and owe only $980 if you pay the invoice within ten days, or you may take up to thirty days and pay the full balance. A terms discount can add up; if you are doing $40,000 a month in invoices, it would save you $800 a month, and over a year it would total $9,600.

Terms are sometimes negotiable with your manufacturers, so be sure to call the credit department and ask. If you are on open terms with your manufacturer, be sure to protect your account at all costs. If you're regularly late with your payments, the credit manager won't hesitate to change your account to a pro forma account. Or worse, they may refuse to ship new product until you've brought your account up to date.

Pro Forma Accounts

With a pro forma account, you are required to pay for the goods you are ordering up front before they will be shipped, much like the way you invoice your client. The downside, as mentioned previously, is that it can slow down your orders while payments are being made. But there is a big plus to a pro forma account, especially for a new business. One of the biggest problems small businesses run into is the "robbing Peter to pay Paul" syndrome. If your cash flow isn't great or you had an unexpected expense, you may find that you are short on funds to pay an invoice when it comes due. Say you had money on hand from Client A who paid you last month for a sofa. The final payment to the manufacturer is now due because you have an open account with a 30-day grace period. But you had car trouble and you had to "borrow" the cash from your checking account and you now don't have those funds. However, Client B has just put in a deposit for window treatments which is enough to cover the sofa bill. So you use those funds to pay the Client A manufacturer's invoice, leaving you short for the Client B invoices. As you can see, this can spiral out of control very quickly. Many a design company has gone out of business and suffered enormous public embarrassment because they let their financial management get out of control. With pro forma accounts, you are much more likely to be using Client A's deposit to pay for their work because the two transactions happen nearly simultaneously. Ultimately, however, as you grow and you have a steady stream of receipts, open accounts will be more controllable and better for your long-term cash flow.

Credit and Your Clients

Many of your jobs, especially to start, may be small, but you may have some that get into the five and six figures. Your job is to outline your prices and fees clearly and your client's job is to pay the bills they have agreed to. You may be tempted to give them terms or ask for smaller deposits because it might make it all more palatable for them. Avoid this thinking and any temptation to do so.

Extending Credit through Your Business

Never extend credit through your business. You don't expect to walk into a jewelry store and ask for them to give you a piece of jewelry with payment due over time.

Your clients will often be better financially fixed than you are and under no circumstances should you make them a loan.

Accepting Credit Cards

Accepting credit cards in your business is perhaps the easiest and best way to help your clients deal with large payments. Many designers report that their sales went up substantially when they started accepting credit cards. This isn't universally the case, though, so it's important to consider this step carefully.

If you think about it, most people use their credit cards to make major purchases, so it stands to reason that if they are buying $3,000 worth of goods, they'll want to use their credit card and pay off the balance as they can.

There are many credit-card servicers out there who all represent the same companies: MasterCard, Visa, Discover, and American Express. The difference is the rates and services that they offer you. Let's start with the most basic item: the credit-card machine. Most of the processing companies will try to sell you a machine outright; those machines can cost hundreds of dollars or more. However, they may also have used machines available for a much lower price. If your budget won't allow you to purchase a machine in the beginning, lease one with an option to buy. A very long-term lease is not worth it because you will be paying the upfront cost many times over if you're in business for a long time—which you will be!

- The best type of machine for this business is the mobile processing machine. It's compact and lightweight, so you can carry it into your customers' home and plug it right into their phone line. You can also use an app provided by your servicer to log in via your computer or if you're running a new version of Quickbooks, you can set up your account system to create an invoice and automatically bill your client's card, with their approval of course. You will be able to verify the card right then, and the process that starts the funds on the way to your bank begins immediately.

- There are alternative ways to accept credit cards as well. PayPal offers online invoicing where you may never actually see your client's credit card. PayPal also offers a mobile card reader attachment for your smart phone so you can take cards on the go. Other similar services exist as well.

Regardless of the company processing your credit card transactions, you need to evaluate the rate that company is charging you. When someone makes a purchase from you and uses a credit card, your processor is going to charge you a fee. Fees range from 1.75 percent all the way up to 6 percent. If you use a processor that charges you 3 percent, your bank statement will show $1,940 on a $2,000 sale ($2,000 – 3% [$60] = $1,940). If you are paying a higher rate of 6 percent, your take from the sale just dropped to $1,880 ($2,000 – 6% [$120] = $1,880). You will usually pay a higher rate to accept the American Express card than the other credit cards. That's why American Express is not always accepted everywhere MasterCard, Visa, and Discover are.

Although it's usually against your contract to add these charges to a sale to make up for the rates you have to pay, no one says that you can't plan for it. If a large percent of your sales are coming from credit-card sales, total the amount that you are paying in fees and work that into your overall selling prices. Much of today's business is conducted with credit cards, and just because you are a small business doesn't mean that you shouldn't be able to compete.

The Real Costs of Accepting Credit Cards

Your client pays you $2,000 for window treatments with a credit card. Your credit card processor retains 3% and deposits the balance to your bank account.

Total Invoice:	$2,000.00
CC fee:	<$60.00>
Net:	$1,940.00
Less fabric and labor invoices:	<$1,300.00>
Your net profit:	$ 640.00

The credit card fee is really closer to 9% of your net profits after you deduct your expenses. If your margins are big—meaning your expenses are low compared to what you charge—it's worth it. But there may be times when your margin is very small—maybe only 10%—and you can end up paying out as much as 30% of your net profit in fees. Not such a bargain for you.

Now that your accounting system is set up, your accounts with the vendors are set up with either open or pro forma terms, and you have researched the various ways to accept payments from your clients, it's time to start setting up your forms and files. Simple things such as bids or estimates, invoices, and vendor files will be covered first. More complicated areas, such as customer contracts and the job tracking worksheet, are described later in this chapter. Let's start with the bid sheet because that's the first piece of paperwork you will generate when you have contact with a customer.

Quotes or Estimate Sheets

Unless what you're selling is easy and straightforward such as an off-the-shelf blind or shade you carry in inventory, you will mostly be creating a quote for your client's approval prior to invoicing. You will find a discussion of the bid sheet and how to use it to sell in chapter 7, but an example of what a simple bid sheet looks like is provided here.

Invoices

Up until the point when a customer commits to giving you a down payment, the only paperwork you will have are your notes pertaining to the customer's styles, colors, and measurements. You may have furniture style preferences or fabric swatches in a file with the customer's name on it, but as far as company paper-work goes, the invoice will be the beginning of the real paper trail. Even a quote or estimate isn't "real" in the sense that they don't hit your books or create a receivable until converted to an invoice. If you're using an accounting software package, standard form invoices will be built in. You will be able to customize these invoices with your logo, company name, contact information, and other pertinent details. Standard spreadsheet and word processing applications such as Microsoft Office or Apple's iWork software come with readymade templates that you can edit as needed. If you want to present a professional image, try to avoid handwritten invoices.

Client Files

Because of all the information you will gather on each client and the amount of details you will have to remember, it's important that your client files be well maintained and organized. In them you will keep all the measurements, the fabric swatches or fabric names to be used on the job, time schedules for each project you're working on, and any special instructions. In addition to these details, you will keep the obvious client information on a sheet in the front of the file. Such information should include the client's name, address, phone number, email, type of work, product selections, method of payment, and so on. A simple file folder may work for basic jobs, but for large, ongoing projects, many designers use a three-ring binder with plastic sleeves to keep their client details organized. This becomes your "bible" for this client and your historical record into the future.

We discussed earlier in this chapter why it's imperative to sign a contract with the client before starting any job. Now let's examine what to put in that contract.

The first section of the contract is where you determine who is who. This is where you will establish what everyone will be called and what the location of

Sample Quote

Date _____

Customer _____

Address _____

Phone Number (Home) _____

Phone Number (Work) _____

Email _____

Product/Description _____

_____

Rooms and Sizes_____

_____

Price $ _____

Tax $ _____

Total $ _____

Prices Good Until _____

the job is. For instance, you can call your client the homeowner, and yourself the contractor or designer. From there you will get into the more specific rules of the contract.

The first issue you should address in your contract is the fact that the order is custom. The customer should understand that with custom orders, returns and cancellations are not allowable. Once an order is placed and in progress, it can't be cancelled without penalties. If the customer decides to cancel the order before it's in production, you should still assign a fee (such as 10 percent of the order) as a cancellation fee to cover the time and expenses you have already put into the job.

Next, you need to protect yourself from the back orders and drops that will occur in your vendor lines. A back order occurs when the vendor you are ordering from has not received the product from the mill. A drop occurs when the mill decides to replace a style or color with one that it thinks will sell better. Once a product has been dropped, it is not available anymore. A simple statement relieving you of any obligation toward an exact delivery date is important to guard against delays caused by back orders and drops.

As a designer, you will be giving out advice on colors, styles, and so much more. Sometimes clients will be unhappy when they see the final result, even after you have drawn the design and shown them samples, photos, and floor plans. But final decisions are always their responsibility and the contract should so state. There can also be a problem with dye lots in some fabric, wallpaper, and carpet samples and with various wood products. With these samples, there is a possibility that the actual finished product will vary slightly in color. The contract should relieve you of any obligation in this regard as well. It's important to note that you should always order a cutting for approval before you accept an order of fabric. You can check this against your sample to be sure the goods you will be receiving match. If not, ask for a different dye lot or your client may have to select a different fabric.

Your returned-check charge should be stated in the contract. Find out what your bank will charge you if one of your customers gives you a bad check. Pass this fee along to the customer with $5 or $10 added to it for your time and expense in collecting it.

To avoid any confusion, your contract should state that all product sold will be separately invoiced and upon approval from the client. Payment of the invoice constitutes approval. You never want to be in a position where the clients think they ordered one thing, or agreed to one price and you think it's something else.

A final suggestion for your contract is a clause stating that the prevailing party in a legal battle will be entitled to all costs and attorney fees. Such a provision may keep clients from filing frivolous lawsuits.

A sample contract follows: it is given only as an example. Always have an attorney help you with your contract so that you are following local laws.

Job Tracking Worksheet

A job tracking worksheet is perhaps one of the most important tools that you will use in your business. It will help you keep track of your customers and their orders, whether or not you have been paid, the estimated delivery date, the date of installation, the date the invoice is due to the vendor or contractor, and when it was paid. It will tell you how much commission is due to your employees, how much the contractor labor amounted to, and more. If you have a computer, you can run your weekly, monthly, and even yearly totals with a couple of keystrokes. Even if you don't have a computer, I highly recommend using this sheet and filling in the blanks manually.

A sample worksheet follows. With this system, you can list each specific order of the job separately. If you want to pull up the entire job file on your computer, simply type in the SM, and everything relating to that customer's name will appear. Also provided are detailed explanations of the column headers so you can see what each abbreviation means and how to fill in the blanks.

Date _____ Invoice No. _____

Dependable Window Coverings and Design
1234 Any Street
Anytown, CA 12345
(555) 555–5555

Salesperson	PO#	Shipped Via	Terms	Estimated Delivery Date

Room   Quantity   Description   Unit Price   Amount

_____

_____

_____

_____

_____

Subtotal $ _____

Sales Tax $ _____

Shipping $ _____

Total $ _____

Deposit Amount $ _____

Balance Due $ _____

All custom sales final—No returns or exchanges.

Thank You!

On this the _____ day of _____, _____, Dependable Window Coverings and Design (contractor or designer) enters a contract with _____ (homeowner) to do the following work at _____.
(What follows should be a detailed description of the project that specifies exactly what work is being done, such as interior design, product specifications, individual products, etc. There should be no ambiguity as to what you have agreed to do for the client, how long it's anticipated to take, and what your fees are).

_____

_____

_____

_____

Anticipated work start date: _____
Anticipated work completion date: _____
Total fee: _____
Payment schedule:

        Deposit: $ _____ due on signing
        Payment #2: $_____ due _____
        Payment #3: $_____ due _____

and so on until the fee is paid in full.

The following terms and conditions apply to the above-mentioned work.

1. All details written on the invoice and signed by the contractor and homeowner shall become part of this contract. Any information given or received over the phone or verbally is not part of the contract.
2. All merchandise sold is custom product and cannot be returned once the order is in progress. If a cancellation does occur before the production of the order has started, the homeowner will be responsible for a 15% cancellation fee. This is to cover time and expenses.
3. There will be a $25 fee for any returned checks.
4. The homeowner is responsible for all final decisions. The contractor will help in the selection but assumes no responsibility for it.
5. Contractor is not responsible for any acts of nature or manufacturer back orders in relationship to product. The delivery dates assigned are estimates and

depend on the availability of the product from the vendor. The contractor will not be liable for any delivery dates scheduled.

6. Certain products will show variances in color and grain. This is typical, and the contractor assumes no liability.

7. The prevailing party shall be entitled to all costs and legal fees in the event of any lawsuit filed by either contractor or homeowner.

8. Freight and installation are included in the total price only if stated on the invoice.

I have read and understand the above terms and conditions for doing business with Dependable Window Coverings and Design. Any questions or concerns have been addressed before entering into this legally binding contract.

Date _____

Homeowner _____   Contractor or Designer _____

Sample Job Tracking Worksheet*

Dependable Interiors Job Tracking Worksheet

Date	PO #	Rep.	SM	Retail	Tax	Tot.	Dep.	Dt. Pd.	Bal. Due.	Dt. Pd.	Vendor	R.E. #	Op.	Del. Dt.

*This chart is an example of the kind of information that might appear on a standard tracking sheet. You will need to create your own tracking system based on the kind of business you are in and what information is necessary to keep on top of.

1. Date. Put the date of the order here.
2. PO #. Use the purchase order number from your invoice here.
3. Rep. This is the space where you will assign the job to a salesperson if you have employees.
4. SM. This is the sidemark, or the customer's last name.
5. Retail. This is the retail price before tax.
6. Tax. This area is for the total sales tax charged.
7. Tot. Combine the retail and sales tax here. This is the column you will use to total your sales figures.
8. Dep. Fill in the amount the customer gave you as a deposit.
9. Dt. Pd. This space is to record the date the customer paid the deposit.
10. Bal. Due. This is the amount the customer owes. You can record a second half of a deposit due here or a balance due from a customer you billed.
11. Dt. Pd. Record here the final payment date of the job.
12. Vendor. This is the manufacturer from whom you've ordered the product for the job. If you have more than one vendor per job, simply fill in the sidemark at the start of the line and skip to this section. Do not fill in the sales price and other data again because it will mess up your monthly and yearly figures.
13. R.E. #. This is the reference number all vendors will give you when you place an order for product.
14. Op. This stands for operator. You should place here the name of the customer service person who took the order. (Not needed when you're a one-person shop.)
15. Del. Dt. This is the delivery date that is promised to you when you place the order.
16. Mini. This and columns 17 through 30 are to be checked if the order contains one or more of the products. For instance, if an order contained twenty-four mini blinds, you would place a 24 in this column. At month's or year's end, you can total the product columns and determine what you are selling the most of and what you need to concentrate more on.
17. Vrt. Vertical blinds.
18. PS. Pleated shade.
19. CP. Crystal pleat.
20. Wd. Wood blind.

21. Shu. Shutter.

22. Top. Top treatment.

23. Fab. Cut fabric.

24. Drp. Custom draperies.

25. Hdwr. Drapery rods or hardware.

26. Crpt. Carpet.

27. Wlpr. Wallpaper.

28. Tile. Tile.

29. Wd. Fl. Wood flooring and related accessories.

30. Misc. Put any product not listed in columns 16 through 29. If you find that you are using a lot of a certain product not listed in those columns, add it to your worksheet with its own column.

31. Cost. Enter your cost of the product here.

32. Inv. #. Put the manufacturer's invoice number here. This will save you a lot of time when they call with questions about a specific invoice.

33. Pd. Enter the date you paid the invoice.

34. Inst. Dt. The date the installation took place goes here.

35. Inst. Amt. Enter the amount you paid to the contractor to have the product installed.

36. BB. This stands for buyback. A buyback is any product that isn't sellable to the customer. If you measure a window wrong and your cost of that shade is $230, it would go in this column. Most of the time the cost of these "Oops!" products are unrecoverable, so this column will be a total of your losses.

37. Rbt. Enter any rebates you get from manufacturers here.

38. Cm. Enter any commission paid here. You will use this column for referral fees and sales commissions.

39. Dt. Pd. Enter the date you paid these commissions.

40. GP. This is your estimated gross profit. Subtract all costs, commissions, installation charges, and buybacks from the sum of the retail plus rebate columns.

Public Relations, Advertising, and Marketing on a Budget

First, it's important to understand the difference between public relations (PR), advertising, and marketing to utilize them efficiently. PR is the process by which one establishes and maintains a positive image with the public. Examples of good PR might be where a company president takes a leadership position in a community organization or sponsors a charitable event. Such activities establish a sense of goodwill among the public. Advertising is the simple task of paying a fee in exchange for promoting one's products or services directly to potential clients such as placement of advertising in a magazine or newspaper or perhaps a television spot. Marketing is, in essence, the overall plan to build awareness of one's products or services and includes both PR and advertising. Marketing is also the process by which we deal with our clients from the start of the relationship, or project, to the end and beyond. Everything we do that offers a positive experience for the client is successful marketing.

Advertising Goals

When you operate a business out of your home, customers will not be walking in off the street to do business with you. People will not drive by your home and realize that there is a business inside. You must rely on unique ways of advertising to attract your potential customers. Marketing is the lifeblood of your business and to be successful, it's an endeavor that should be happening 24/7.

Your ultimate goal should be to build up referral business so that in time you can reduce the costs of your advertising expenses, but in the beginning you will have to heavily rely on marketing and advertising. It's always easier and less expensive to reengage past or current customers than it is to acquire a new one. This chapter presents the typical techniques that most businesses rely on as well as some alternative forms of advertising that are unique to the home-based interior design business. These alternative forms of advertising will also save you money while bringing in the much sought-after business. While some of the larger stores rely on big-dollar advertising forms such as newspaper and television, smaller home-based businesses generally don't have the budget to compete that way. That's where alternative advertising comes in. If you combine the typical advertising methods with the alternative ones in a consistent manner, you may soon have more business than you can handle.

Keep in mind that all the advertising in the world is not a substitute for good old-fashioned customer satisfaction. As stated earlier, referral business is your goal; it decreases your advertising costs and increases your closing rate. (When a customer calls you from a referral, that person is less likely to shop around because someone trusted has recommended your business.) Remember the old shampoo commercial? "I told two friends, and they told two friends, and so on and so on. . . ." Through good referrals, you might end up with work at almost every house on a block. But by the same token, if you have an unsatisfied customer, you will probably not be invited back to any house on that block.

Think of it this way: Advertising is the way to get appointments so that you can sell your products, but your marketing initiatives via excellent customer service and satisfaction is the method in which you will build your business into a long-term profitable venture.

Typical Advertising Techniques

Your Business Brand

Before any type of marketing or advertising takes place, it's essential to create a "look" for your business. Your "look" should represent your design style. This starts with your business name, as discussed in chapter 2, and moves into all visual representations of your business. What does this mean? Everything from your simple little business card to stationery and brochures, print advertising, a website or social media. The font you use, the logo you design, and even the choice of paper all matter. Creating a cohesive "look" across all visual platforms is essential to helping potential clients notice you and remember you. You can hire a professional graphic designer or marketing expert to help guide you in this area. Though it can be expensive, it's a good investment to get it right from the beginning. If this is not possible to start off, then keep it simple, clear, and easy to understand, but above all be consistent. A professional headshot is a very important tool and can be used in both print and online forms, and is a must for anyone in business.

Yellow-Page Ad Placement

Advertising in the Yellow Pages is essentially an old and outdated mode of advertising. Businesses that sell a specific product such as blinds or carpets may see some benefit to keeping up their ads in the phone book but since so few homeowners receive them anymore it doesn't make a lot of sense to spend limited funds in a place few people are looking. An exception to this is the senior citizen market, which is still more likely to check the Yellow Pages for services. If this is one of your target markets, maintaining an ad may serve you well.

Although you will be running an interior design business, you will get most of your calls from yellow-page categories other than interior design. Pick the category from which you want or expect to get most of your business. If you are specializing in window coverings, place your display ad under "Mini Blinds" or "Draperies," and place line ads under the rest of the categories.

If you do decide to invest in Yellow Pages ads, avoid spending money in categories with too much big competition such as carpet, flooring, and wall coverings. A home-based business cannot compete with all the storefronts that specialize in these products and it's a waste of money to pay to compete in those categories. Window coverings and upholstery are easier to promote as you will be offering your services in-home rather than in-store. Additionally, there is more profit margin in these categories and you will have more return on your advertising investment as a result. You will get the carpet and wallpaper sales as a result of doing a total package for your customer.

Business Cards

Business cards are another traditional form of advertising and are usually the first and least expensive method of getting your name out there. Pass them out to anyone and everyone who will accept them. Pin them up on community bulletin boards, leave them lying on restaurant tables, and include them with all your correspondence. Business cards are also one of the least expensive ways of getting your business name in the public eye. As the saying goes, never leave home without them—not even to the dry cleaner or salon.

Don't underestimate the importance of the design of your business card. It should include the important information about your business without looking too crowded. Because of the nature of our business, you can take chances with your cards: the more creative, the better. Your business cards will be a statement of your style. If you have decided that your company colors will be blue and gray, make sure your cards reflect that. If you are going to design a logo for your business, use that on your cards too. Anything that people will recognize as yours will help with name recognition. Extend these ideas to your business stationery, contractor shirts, magnetic car signs, and so on. Make sure everything carries the same theme. As your business grows and you begin to advertise, more people will start to recognize your name. The first time someone tells you that they have heard of your business you'll feel just great. As your name recognition grows, so will your business.

The information that you will want to include on your business cards are the name of your business, your phone number, email address, website address, your name and title, and what services you provide. You may wish to get a PO box or a box at a UPS store that has a real street address to avoid listing your home address publicly.

You will have many different choices when it comes time to purchase your business cards. There are online resources such as vistaprint.com and moo.com that offer very inexpensive business cards. You can use one of their templates or upload your own. If you haven't developed your brand's "look" yet, select a template that is clean and attractive—it's more important to start getting your name out there. In other words, while your brand's "look" is important, don't let the lack of it stop you from having business cards right from the get-go.

DEPENDABLE WINDOW COVERINGS AND DESIGN

CUSTOM SERVICE AT GREAT PRICES
Window Coverings • Flooring • Wallpaper
Upholstery • Draperies • Design Consultation

Your Name Here
Owner/Designer
555-555-5555 www.myweburl.com
Free In-Home Estimates

Website

It is absolutely imperative to have a website these days. If you're not online, you don't exist. And this is doubly true for an at-home business. Only the most established, old-school designers can get away without a website and even they are struggling to acquire new clients. Food for thought: email has been around since the early 1990s and Amazon launched in 1995. An entire generation of people have only known life online. According to a 2013 Pew research study, only 15 percent of American adults report not using the internet at all. If 85 percent of our potential client base is online, how can we not be? Designer websites come in all styles and levels of complexity but the good news is that we don't need a fancy, huge website to get the job done. Focus on the basics of storytelling: who, what, where, when, and why. Who are you, what do you do, where are you located and how can you be reached, when are you available, and why are you better than your competition? Answer all those questions, include professional photos of your work or products you offer, make it easy for the prospect to contact you, and you are on your way. At the start of this chapter, the notion of marketing 24/7 was mentioned. This is where your website brings its real value. We're all browsing online at all hours of the day and night looking for products and services. As a home-based business, we don't want to be fielding telephone calls during our "off hours"—this is the purpose of our website. A caveat: Your website is your electronic brochure and represents your "brand." Do not leave it to your college-age child to do it for you— they may have technological skills but will not have any idea how to create and maintain a professional image.

Social Media

Embedded within its name is the core to social media—it's about being social and establishing a personal connection. It's the online equivalent of the water cooler in the office or the back yard fence at home. In the ten years since Facebook was founded, an entirely new way to communicate and promote our businesses and services has grown up. The upside is that most of these marketing opportunities are free. The downside is that they do take a certain amount of time and willing-ness to learn a small bit of technology. It's not hard, but it takes focus. The biggest complaint is that people say they don't have time to spend all day online or that it's only for young people. Yet some very successful designers have built their busi-nesses around their social media savvy by staying top of mind with regular posts about their projects, interests, and travels, and building a following. According to a Pew research study released in September 2013, over 65 percent of college-educated women between the ages of 50 and 65 who are in households with incomes greater than $75,000 are users of social networking sites. That's a lot of potential clients.

One of the biggest secrets is that all of the journalistic media today is online and heavily involved with social media. Want to connect directly with a local jour-nalist who specializes in home decor stories? Or how about the editor-in-chief of your favorite shelter magazine? They are all online and welcome the connections. Social media has completely broken down the walls between designers, manufacturers, the media, and consumers. Even if you don't get clients directly from your social media activities, though many do, it's likely that you will make industry connections that will open doors to potential clients and more exclusive resources. Another little-known use for social media sites are the private groups that are using their platforms to allow industry peers to connect and network among each other in a secure setting. You can gain industry insights or just share your frustrations without the wider public seeing what you're talking about. For those in a home-based business, online networking is a great way to stay connected without having to leave home.

So the question you may have is where to start and what will work best? There are many different social media sites and it can be difficult to keep up with what's "best." Ultimately, the best option for you is the one you feel comfortable with and will stick to. Do you need to be "on" every waking minute? Not at all. But you do need to be consistent. Here are highlights of some of the most popular sites for the interior design industry. See appendix A for URLs and information.

- Facebook with its billion-plus users is clearly the big player on the social media stage. Think of it like a big bulletin board where you pin up your news, also known as *posts* or *status updates*. When you look at your "wall," you will see the latest posts by those you follow, the most recent first. Your friends, or connections, will see your news as well. Personal pages are interactive between friends and are meant to be like chatting over the back yard fence or meeting up at a college reunion. Facebook also offers business pages where you post your news and develop followers who are interested in knowing what the latest is for your business. It's less interactive and can take a while to develop a following, but it's an excellent free source of marketing and can serve as an interim (and free!) website until yours is up and running. The downside to Facebook is that they often update the look of the pages, how things are done, and who sees which posts. It can be hard to keep up, but it doesn't look like Facebook is going anywhere anytime soon so is worth consideration. There are also many private interior design groups on Facebook who share information and ideas with colleagues from around the country and the globe.

- LinkedIn is similar to Facebook but has always been more business focused. It's not unlike attending your college reunion where what you do professionally is the most important information you are sharing and personal life stories come second.

- Twitter has been compared to walking into a bar and mingling with a crowd of people—some you know and some you don't. A few words here and a few there and then you're on your way. The power of Twitter is that it's quick and easy, and with its 140-character limit, it forces us to learn to get our messages out there succinctly. You can use Twitter to promote a sale you're having or updates to your website and portfolio.

- Instagram is much like a visual Twitter. You post a picture of where you are, what you're working on, even what you're eating. Yes, even though you are a professional, there is room for a little personal information as well. After all, we like to work with people we like. Be likable and personable and you will find how easy it is to make connections. Interior design is a visual and creative field, so take advantage of the opportunity to showcase your work quickly and efficiently.

- Pinterest is another "bulletin" board type of medium. Much like magazine pages that we stuff into file folders or on a pin board, Pinterest allows you to "pin" images into different folders for future reference. Designers use it to catalogue products they are considering for clients as well as to showcase their style and taste—even if the photos aren't their own work. You can follow other users' boards as well and see what they are interested in. Some designers who were early adopters of Pinterest have over a million followers!

- Blogs (short for "web log") started out as personal online journals and many still are. They are your own space on the internet to talk about whatever you wish to discuss. You can use a blog to post about your product lines, offer advice on various topics such as how to measure for fabric repeats, or tips on styling a room for under $100. Your blog is your personal calling card and should always reflect your brand. If your target clientele is the high-end luxury market, you may wish to focus on posting about travel and world-class resorts, high-end products, and the like. You may wish to avoid DIY projects or low-cost budget tips. On the other hand, if your market is more middle of the road, then speak to those needs. You can use your blog to showcase projects you are working on or have just completed; you control the message. We no longer need to wait for a magazine or newspaper to write about us to be published! While it's important to post on a consistent basis, that may be once a week or maybe only twice a month, or it could be daily. It's about quality, not just quantity. A great value of a blog is that internet search engines such as Google and Bing value regularly updated websites over static sites. Our business websites do tend to be static (sitting out there with few updates) and can show up lower in search results. A regularly updated website such as a blog will come up higher in a search. If your blog is linked to your website, or better yet a part of your website, you will benefit greatly.

A caveat to always keep in mind when it comes to the internet and social media is this: Everything you post remains online in some form forever. A political rant, a photo, a negative comment about a client, or negativity in general. Everything we do online speaks to who we are and can affect our business prospects.

Print Advertising

If you are planning to advertise in the newspaper or a local shelter or lifestyle magazine, you must make a long-term commitment to it. Running an ad once or twice is not going to bring you much business; it will mostly be a waste of money and effort. Print advertising can be expensive depending on where you live. In most of the larger cities, the cost of advertising in one of the large newspapers is usually out of the question for most home-based businesses, especially a startup.

There are plenty of different options out there. Small-town newspapers are much less expensive than regional papers. "Shopper's News" type papers are an option, but they are very bargain oriented and you will need to be prepared to offer some kind of discount or bargain as part of your advertisement. This is where the loss-leader theory comes in. If your primary business is product oriented, rather than service, you can advertise a single product such as mini blinds at a substantial discount, and then once you get into the customer's home, you can suggest more profitable items such as shutters or draperies and more. As a design consultant, all you have are your ideas to sell and it doesn't usually pay off to give too much away. You might offer a limited service such as a color consultation and then if the client wishes more, they will pay your standard rates. The idea is to get into the home and build a relationship with the customer. Only then can you make your best sale.

Other options for print advertising are community newspapers or newsletters. Some subdivisions or small communities will have a newsletter dedicated to the issues of their community. They may sell advertising space in their newsletters very inexpensively. If you live in one of these communities, you should absolutely be advertising in that newsletter, but you can also advertise in the ones for communities that you don't live in. Using this type of advertising may bring you quite a bit of business for a minimal investment. When you place an ad in one of these newsletters, make a special offer to that community, perhaps a percentage discount off a product or an introductory free hour of design consultation. If you are advertising in the Oakwood Farms Private Homeowners Association, your ad might look something like the following sample.

Sample Community Newsletter Advertisement

Special Offer for
Oakwood Farms Residents ONLY!
Receive 50% off a Color Consultation OR
Free Lining with Any Custom Drapery Purchase.
Dependable Window Coverings and Design
555-555-5555 • www.mywebURL.com

Television and Radio

Television advertising is expensive if you advertise in a time slot when people are watching and why would you want to advertise any other time? Generally speaking, TV advertising is just too expensive and won't produce the kinds of results that other, less expensive forms of advertising will. Radio advertising is also questionable. It's likely that listeners are driving in their cars when listening, so they may tune out ads or simply not be able to write down your information. Additionally, it's hard to track your results from radio or television because many people won't even remember where they heard your name. As with print advertising, radio and television ads are good for name recognition when used over an extended period, but they are less successful generating immediate results. Local stations, however, may offer special opportunities such as community sponsorships that may not be too expensive and may result in multiple mentions of your business name. It's worth looking into if you have such a local station.

Mailing Lists

Direct mail campaigns are certainly a way to get your information right into the hands of potential clients. However, most campaigns have a response rate of approximately 1 to 2 percent with a huge success being 3 percent. Email campaigns are trickier than print mail. While they are certainly less expensive with no print or postage expenses, there are strict antispam laws in place that must be followed. All direct email should be permission based, which can be hard to obtain. Search on line for the CAN-SPAM Act for more information.

You can purchase mailing lists from list brokers by whatever category you choose for print mail but it's not allowed for emails. List brokers, which you can find online, offer lists by income, subdivisions, even by people who have recently bought a new home. Just be sure it's a reputable broker whose lists aren't old and out of date or you'll be receiving a lot of "return to sender" pieces, which is a big waste of your money. New home sales transactions are also routinely included in local papers as well if you wish to create your own lists. If you're selling window products such as blinds and shutters you may see good results with this market. We all need privacy in our bedrooms and bathrooms.

As mentioned previously, email campaigns must be permission based but a good list of interested readers can be a great source of business. Check appendix A for a list of reputable services who will also help you follow the CAN-SPAM laws. You can gather emails by using sign-up boxes on your website or Facebook pages, your client base, business associates, friends, and family. Since it's easy to forward an email, your list will continue to grow over time.

Telemarketing

We have all been assaulted by telemarketers. Federal and state laws in effect since 2003 govern this practice. Before you decide to telemarket, check with your State Attorney General's office and the Federal Trade Commission. Be current on what you can and cannot do regarding telemarketing for new business.

When someone suggests you call one of his or her friends, you should ask that person to tell the prospect you will be calling in a few days. The future client will be more receptive to your call if he or she is already expecting it. This is really a referral, and will probably end up being the most popular way you'll get new business. No amount of advertising or telemarketing can beat a referral from a satisfied client!

Magnetic Car Signs

Another advertising option is to go to a sign shop and order two magnetic signs to place on the side doors of your car. They should also be brief and to the point. Some people are troubled by this type of advertising because it could possibly put you in a vulnerable position. After all, you are not only exposing your business to the public, but also giving people a glance at you, too (along with your phone number). Conceivably, this could make you a target for crank calls or other unwanted mischief. If this possibility doesn't disturb you, a magnetic car sign is an inexpensive way to put your business name in the public eye. Just don't drive like a maniac and promote *bad* feelings about your company. It's also important to note that local laws may dictate that any signage, even temporary magnetic signs, on an automobile makes it a commercial vehicle which requires special registration and more expensive insurance coverage. On the plus side, you will be able to park in commercial zones, which may be a real plus depending on where you're located.

Brochures

Brochures are an excellent way to promote your business and are designed with the idea of selling the products and services you have to offer. Unless you have a desktop publishing program and a laser printer, you will likely pay about $1,500 for the design and printing of quality brochures. Some manufacturers offer brochures for their specific product lines, but they only promote that manufacturer's products and are generally too generic. As your business grows and it is in the budget, a brochure can be a useful form of advertising. Brochures are also a great marketing tool for commercial clients or high-end residential clients. When calling on architects, remodelers, or Realtors, a quality brochure will make a solid first impression. If you're going to make the investment in a four-color print brochure, it may be wise to hire a graphic designer who can lay it out and format the text and images properly for the best printing results.

Associations and Networking

Go to as many meetings as you can and pass out your business cards. Don't go to these meetings and just stand around waiting for something to happen because it rarely will. Remember the reason you are there: to increase your business. However, don't just talk; effective networking means listening as well. Everyone at a networking meeting is there to sell his or her own products and services and to increase his or her business. It goes both ways and nothing is more of a turn off than someone who presses the flesh and tosses around their cards without a care for the person he or she is speaking with. It's a numbers game, but it's quality numbers, not mere quantity. Networking organizations are also a great way to learn how to talk about your business and to practice your "elevator pitch" especially if you're new in business. Becoming involved by joining committees and taking a leadership role in the organization will also help get your name out there. You are more likely to be dealing with higher level business professionals who also gravitate toward leadership positions.

Allied Professional Marketing

Networking and getting the word out about your business is a relationship game. Allied professionals are those whom you are not in direct competition with but who serve the same client base. Examples of these are architects, builders, and Realtors. Ask for a meeting to see if there are mutual benefits to working with each other. You might offer a Realtor a discount on home-staging services if that's a line of work you wish to pursue. You could even simply offer to sponsor a Realtor's Open House or Caravan when a new house hits the market. You'd be providing the lunch for a group of real estate professionals and do some in-person networking. Not everyone you reach out to will be interested in your pitch, so just keep moving on. The important point is to make it worth it for both parties.

You will need to be prepared to be persistent when cold-calling a prospect. Leave a brochure and card the first time you visit, then call and make sure they got it. Call and try to set up an appointment with the manager of the office. Be clear about your purpose and promise to not take too much time. If you get a meeting, write a thank-you note afterward. If you don't hear back, put the lead on your mailing list and send periodic reminders about what you do.

One more way to endear yourself to these potential clients is to be willing to tackle emergency jobs that other companies won't want to touch. Perhaps a vertical blind needs repair, and your profit on the job would be only $15. Most companies would beg off, claiming that their schedule was full. Take the job, and the next one sent your way may be a lot more substantial. They will appreciate your helping them out of a bind and will remember you the next time they have a job.

Job Site Signs

Lawn signs work well if you are doing a large job in a neighborhood you wish to be doing more business in. It's customary for builders and architects to do so, so why not the designer? You can have these foam board signs made up for approximately $30 to $50 each. The more you buy, the less they will cost. You will have to ask your clients' permission to leave the sign in their yard, of course, and if they agree, leave it for only a week or two. Yard signs can be an inexpensive way of letting all of your clients' neighbors know your name.

Contractor Shirts

When anyone representing your company goes to one of your clients' homes, they should dress professionally. You can promote your company image by requiring that your contractors wear work shirts with your company name, logo, and phone number on them. You should provide each worker with two shirts in case one of them gets dirty. The shirts can be T-shirts or collared shirts; just make sure they are neat and have your company name and phone number in large, bold letters on them.

Home Shows

Once or twice a year in every major U.S. city, home shows are held in the local convention center. If your city isn't large enough to have a home show, you can bet that something similar will be held at one of the local shopping malls. A home show is an event where retailers show off their wares. They rent spaces in booths and set up displays that they hope will make the shoppers want to do business with them. There are many sizes of booths to choose from, and they vary greatly in cost. A 10-foot-square booth is a good size. Bigger booths might attract a little more attention, but not enough to justify the cost. Just make sure your smaller booth is eye-catching. It should encourage the shoppers to stop and find out what you have to offer. This is an expensive proposition, however, and you need to carefully consider the location and potential foot traffic. Your costs will include the space rental, which can run from hundreds to tens of thousands of dollars. You will have to create a booth from floor to ceiling, stock the booth with brochures and samples, and staff the booth as well. Carefully weigh the cost against the potential income.

The great thing about home shows is that almost everyone there is looking for something for their home or building a new one. Your goal once again is to set up as many in-home appointments as you can. Do this by offering a one-time sale good only for people who set up an appointment at the show. Once the home show is over, you should be extremely busy for the next couple of weeks fulfilling these meetings and following up on any other leads that may have been generated. Just remember that you are only one person and you may have existing clients that you need to be servicing. Plan your time accordingly.

Trunk Shows

People love a party and to see what's fresh and new. Host a luncheon or afternoon tea and invite your neighbors over to learn about the new fabric or window treatment trends. Talk with your fabric sales rep about offering a "one day only" special rate on new orders placed. You can hand out brochures at the party that detail the type of work that you do, which should spark some interest in the other services that you offer such as wallpaper or reupholstery.

Advertising on the Internet

Depending on whether you use your website to sell products or just display your company information, you may or may not want to use the following forms of advertising:

- **Banner ads.** Exchanging banner links with other like businesses, such as landscapers or florists, will increase the number of visitors to your site.

Trade Show Tips

- Have a dry run. Set up your booth in your garage or backyard and invite friends, family, and even good customers to preview it and give you suggestions.

- Have everyone working the booth dress in the same colors (your corporate colors perhaps) or in your contractor shirts if you use them. This will give your booth a more uniform, professional look.

- Think high, not wide. Trade shows are usually held in large convention centers, and it's easy to get lost among the hundreds of booths, but even the smallest exhibitors can get noticed by building their booth up. Do this by purchasing the tallest back drape you can, and then adding a sign or banner on top of that.

- If you have employees, prepare them. Make sure they know their goals—setting appointments, getting people to register for the giveaway, and so on. Role-playing can be an effective way to ensure that everyone knows his or her job.

- Perform frequent demonstrations at your booth to attract a crowd. Then draw them in with your knowledge and charm!

- Put plenty of chairs in your booth. Shoppers have been on their feet all day, so why not let them sit in your booth and have a drink or snack, or better yet, a professional foot massage? Just don't sit in the chairs yourself. Nothing says "I don't care" like a booth attendant who is sitting down ignoring the passersby.

But be careful about placing too many banners on your site, because you want the consumer to see your product, not just a bunch of flashing banners. Also, thoroughly research every organization that you represent on your site, because it will be a direct reflection of you and your company. (Likewise, don't agree to advertise your company on a website that doesn't meet your standards.)

- **Write articles.** By writing and submitting articles about your specialty, you will become known as an expert in the field, and that can only increase your business. You can submit these articles to other like sites, targeted e-zines (online magazines that appeal to homeowners), or attach them to your own site.

- **Search engine placement.** A lot has been written on the subject of how to get ranked at the top of search engines. The problem is that most search engines have different rules for placement, they change quite frequently, and they punish companies (by lowering your page rank) who look like they have been trying to game the system by paying for placement. Ultimately, the best way to achieve a high search engine ranking is to keep your content fresh and target your keywords to your desired location and business demographic.

Other Ways to Get Business

Reading the Newspaper

This isn't exactly a form of advertising, but it *is* a way to get business. Keeping up with what's going on in town may net you some interesting jobs that might not otherwise come your way. Perhaps a local museum or nonprofit is busy fundraising so they can build a new addition. Find out who will be hiring contractors or making finish selections and ask what the process is to be considered. It sometimes takes a bit of creative thinking, but there are many opportunities right under our noses.

Becoming an Expert

You can gain recognition as an expert in a variety of ways. One of them is to send press releases to newspapers and radio stations every time you or your business accomplishes a goal. This goal could include anything from completing a job at a local business to hiring a new employee.

Holding seminars about your specialty will certainly put you in the public eye. If you become a specialist at window coverings, hold a seminar on how to select the right fabrics for different types of applications. Let the word out that you are available for speeches at the local design school (and then issue a press release) or volunteer to write a design column in your local or community newspaper. If you do regularly send out press releases, make sure to post them on your own website as well. The keywords in the press release will help the search engines find you.

Tracking Your Business

One of the most important rules of advertising is to keep track of where your business comes from. You may try many of the different advertising methods provided here, and probably a few more you'll come up with on your own. Each community is different, and it's hard to tell which form of advertising will attract most of your business. If you use an advertising tracking system, there will be no guesswork involved, and you will save hundreds or even thousands of advertising dollars every year. Whenever you get an inquiry call, whether it turns into a job or not, ask callers where they heard about you and then make a note of it in your advertising tracking log. See the sidebar for an example of the type of information you will want to track. There is a line titled "Jobs?" Mark an X in the "Yes" space if the call turns into a job and in the "No" space if it doesn't. When tabulating your results, keep in mind that it will tell you where the "shoppers" and the serious callers are coming from. If you've had thirty calls from one ad but only two of those people bought from you, unless they were large jobs, you might not want to run that ad again. On the other hand, if you've had five calls from another ad and four out of those five people bought from you, that's an ad you will want to run again. Tracking isn't something that you should do only when just starting your business. Rather, it will help you plan and keep track of your advertising for the life of your business.

Seminar Tips

- Rent a meeting room at a hotel or motel to achieve a professional atmosphere. You might also seek space in a local showroom or storefront of an allied professional, which is good marketing for both of you.

- Advertise and plan weeks earlier. If you haven't done much public speaking, practice in front of friends and family, and take suggestions on how it could be more fun and educational.

- Offer the seminar for free, and then offer a special discount to anyone who sets an appointment that day.

- Provide simple refreshments. You want the attendees to be comfortable. A local caterer or baker may be willing to offer free treats in exchange for their business getting a mention to the right crowd.

- Have product on site to sell such as drapery hardware or small custom soft goods like pillows.

- Be high energy, and make it fun. You'll probably do more of these, and you want the customers telling their friends about it.

- At the end of the seminar, ask participants to fill out an anonymous critique. This will allow you to get honest feedback so you can improve each time.

- Keep track of sales so you'll know whether or not the seminar is bringing you enough sales to justify the effort.

DATE _____   CUSTOMER _____

ADVERTISING SOURCE _____

KEYWORDS USED IF INTERNET SEARCH _____

NOTES _____

JOB?   Y _____   N _____

JOB VALUE $ _____

DATE _____   CUSTOMER _____

ADVERTISING SOURCE _____

KEYWORDS USED IF INTERNET SEARCH _____

NOTES _____

JOB?   Y _____   N _____

JOB VALUE $ _____

DATE _____   CUSTOMER _____

ADVERTISING SOURCE _____

KEYWORDS USED IF INTERNET SEARCH _____

NOTES _____

JOB?   Y _____   N _____

JOB VALUE $ _____

DATE _____   CUSTOMER _____

ADVERTISING SOURCE _____

KEYWORDS USED IF INTERNET SEARCH _____

NOTES _____

JOB?   Y _____   N _____

JOB VALUE $ _____

Using Existing Clients to Cultivate New Business

After a while, your largest source of new business will be sitting right there in your files: your former clients. Repeat business is a wonderful compliment; it means someone liked your work enough to hire you again.

Your former clients may not always call you, however; sometimes they may not even realize that they need to update their colors or styles. It's your job to remind them of that. There are several ways you can do so. The newsletter that you send out will be a constant reminder to your clients that you are consistently keeping up-to-date on new products and services. You can also make periodic phone calls, about every six months, just to find out if they are in the market for anything or simply to just "catch up."

Holidays are a great time to remind former clients of your business. Send cards to all of your former and present clients. Handwrite every one of them—it will make a bigger impact. Keep track of past clients' birthdays and anniversaries. A surprise note in the mail will really grab their attention.

Some of your former clients will sell their homes and move to new ones, or make additions or changes to their existing ones. By keeping in contact with these former clients, chances are good that they will call you to do additional work when that time comes. One of the biggest reasons for keeping in touch with your old clients is the referrals that they can send you. They work in offices or stores and have friends and relatives; all of these people at one time or another will require your services. It is important to remember that you do need to ask for their referral. Say something like, "I loved working with you on your project and I am always looking for more clients just like you. If you can think of anyone who may need my product or services, I would so appreciate the referral." It's simple and flattering.

One way to cultivate client referrals is to offer your existing clients something tangible in return for sending you business. You could offer them a discount on any work that they plan to do in the future based on how much business their referrals bring in. For instance, give them a $25 gift certificate for every $1,000 that they send you in business. The advantage to using this system is that the gift certificates alone probably won't cover the cost of the future job; it just offers them an incentive to continue working with you.

After every job is finished, you should follow up with a handwritten thank-you note and even a gift if the project was large enough. This small gesture goes a long way in creating goodwill between you and your client. And of course, you will be keeping the client on your mailing lists for your monthly newsletters and holiday greetings, keeping you top of mind.

Keeping Track of Your Clients

This all sounds great, you say, but how do I keep track of all my old clients? It can be done several ways. You can keep a client file on your computer in database or even just spreadsheet format. Include First Name, Last Name, Address, City, State, Zip, work and home telephone numbers, email address, and information about what they bought from you. This will come in handy when you want to do something like mail out your newsletters: Simply transfer that file into your mail merge and your computer will print out your labels for you.

In addition to the basic information, such as your clients' names, addresses, email and phone numbers, you will want to keep track of the work done in their homes and any work that you know they may want done in the future. To keep an ongoing relationship with your clients, you'll also need to keep track of when and why you last had contact with them. A very simple method is this: When you have completed a job and are ready to file the client folder away, staple the client tracking sheet to the outer front cover of the folder. You want the sheet on the outside of the file folder because it will save you time when you are going through your files. You won't have to pull every one of them out and open them up; you can simply flip through them. Go through your files once a month to determine who needs a reminder of your services. Predetermine a period of time that should pass between phone calls or letters, perhaps six months in the beginning and once a year after that. The sample client tracking sheet provided on page 92 should prove helpful. There are also many software applications available for client management that house all of your information in one place. As your business grows you will likely wish to move from paper to easier-to-manage computer files.

Turning Inquiry Calls into Sales

When someone calls you with questions about pricing or services, you have an ideal opportunity for a sale. Your goal will be to determine what the person is looking for and if he or she is the right client for your services. The first thing you will have to do is qualify the person, that is, determine whether or not the person is really ready to make a purchase and is the right client for you. Some of the questions you may ask the caller are:

- How soon are you looking at having the work complete?

- Are you planning on doing work in one room or many?

- Have you determined a budget for this project?

April 10, 2014

Dear Susie:

I want to thank you once again for your business. If I can be of service to you in the future, I hope you will not hesitate to call. In the meantime, I have enclosed a few of my business cards. I would greatly appreciate it if you would consider referring my services to friends and family. I hope you are enjoying your new surroundings, and call me if I can be of any help.

Warmly,
[Your signature here]
[Your typed name here]

Sample Client Tracking Sheet

Name _____

Address _____

Phone number   (h) _____   (o) _____   m) _____

Email _____

Start date of job _____

End date of job _____

Work or service provided _____

_____

Work still to be done _____

Reason not done _____

Client satisfied with work? _____

Date of contact _____   Reason _____   Response _____

Date of contact _____   Reason _____   Response _____

Date of contact _____   Reason _____   Response _____

Date of contact _____   Reason _____   Response _____

Date of contact _____   Reason _____   Response _____

Date of contact _____   Reason _____   Response _____

Date of contact _____   Reason _____   Response _____

Date of contact _____   Reason _____   Response _____

Date of contact _____   Reason _____   Response _____

Date of contact _____   Reason _____   Response _____

If the caller has definite answers to these questions, that means that the person has thought it through and is probably ready to make a purchase. If the caller's answers aren't certain, he or she may just be shopping around. If this is the case, always be kind and courteous and answer their questions clearly. When the time comes for them to buy, they will remember the business who took the time to answer their questions. You might also ask if they would like to be included on your mailing list by leaving their information. If your caller has answered the first round of questions confidently, then you will want to proceed by setting up an in-home meeting to further determine the scope of the project.

After you have established the time and place, you still need to ask a few more questions so that you will arrive at the appointment prepared. In addition to preparing you, those questions will also instill confidence in your prospective client by making the caller feel you are taking his or her needs seriously and will work hard to fill them. The following questions would be appropriate if the caller were inquiring about draperies; adjust your questions according to the type of product or service that your caller is interested in.

- What room or rooms do you want draperies for?

- How many windows are involved?

- What is your style and color scheme? Do you want to change it or stay with it?

- Will you need new drapery rods or do you want to use the existing ones?

- Would you like for me to bring along coordinating upholstery fabrics or wallpaper?

- Are the draperies to be used for function or beauty? If beauty, do you also need to see some mini blinds, verticals, or shades?

By the time you hang up the phone, you will know whether the customer is interested in one balloon valance or a house full of draperies with a possibility of additional upholstery and cellular shade work. Knowledge is power. Use the phone calls as a way to establish a rapport with your client, and get the information you need to appear like the professional that you are. Since more and more inquiries are coming via email, you will want to set up a phone call to run your qualifying process as outlined above. Many interior designers and decorators also request prospects to fill out a questionnaire on their websites or that is sent via email, which covers all of the previous information and more. Prospects who are willing to take these extra steps are generally more ready to move forward than those who aren't. Whether in writing or via a phone conversation, the goal is to make sure the prospect is potentially worth the time you will spend meeting in their home. Wasting precious time meeting with someone who isn't really all that interested is lost money.

What to Charge

In chapter 1 we discussed the differences between a consultation designer and a product-oriented professional whose profits largely come from the sale of products. Whether charging for your time as a consulting designer or charging only for product, how you charge will make or break your business model. If you're a design consultant, your hourly rate is usually determined in part by how much experience you have, your geographic area and really, simply, by how much people are willing to pay you. Product sales can seem like a more straightforward process because often there is a stated "list" or "suggested retail price" on the product and you can either charge that price, or offer whatever discounts you wish. But of course it's really not that simple.

You will also learn, step by step, the way through the maze of giving an estimate or bidding on a project. There may be times when you will be asked to match or beat a competitor's bid. You will need to be able to take apart that bid to determine what grade of product is being sold and for how much. For instance, what if a customer handed you a bid from a competitor for twenty-four bamboo shades and asked you to match it? Before agreeing, you would first need to determine whether or not you actually can match the pricing. If your competition is a big box store or a larger design shop, they will most certainly have better buyer power that you do in your one-person, at-home business. While you don't have their overhead, they are likely buying the same products at such substantially lower prices that you will never be able to match their pricing product to product without losing your shirt. What to do? The answer is sometimes you just can't match the bid. And other times, it's that the level of service and design advice you can offer simply makes your products worth the higher price.

Understanding who your competition is and how they operate is an important first step if you're selling products that are easily available around town. If you're a consulting designer, you should also be researching the other designers in your area, how they work, and what services they provide.

Getting to Know Your Competition

If you are going to be successful in any business in the retail and sales sectors, it's essential to know who your competition is, how they operate and how you can differentiate yourself to stand out from the crowd. The more information you can glean will be helpful as you establish your target market, your pricing, and even what products and services you will be offering. Getting that information is a matter of research. Presumably, you already know some of these businesses; you may have even purchased from them in the past. Online searches and telephone listings will also help in your research.

Once you have determined who your competition is, you will need to get more specific information. Looking at their websites will offer a wealth of information (it will also give you great ideas for what your own website should look like). For instance, most companies will list the products and manufacturers that they sell, as well as their customer-service policies, shipping time, and much more.

Look for other clues into your competitors' makeup, such as their hours of operation, whether or not they accept credit cards, if they work out of a home or an office (people who work out of their homes usually don't list a physical address), and any special offerings such as complimentary measuring and installations. Designer's websites most often will include the types of work they do and the size of the projects they take, and some even list their fees. Check out their portfolios to learn what styles they specialize in or types of spaces such as kitchens and baths versus living rooms. If you're going to be a products-driven business, the work-sheet provided on page 98 can help you keep track of your competitors' prices and the manufacturers that they use. Fill out a separate worksheet for each competitor. Use a separate line on the sheet for each product.

From the sample advertisement on page 97, you could determine that Bill's Home Emporium's focus product is window coverings and that Graber is his preferred manufacturer. He also probably gets co-op money from Graber—that is, Graber pays part of the cost for Bill's ad because it mentions Graber products, a technique called *cooperative,* or *co-op, advertising.* Bill's also sells a variety of other products. Bill obviously likely works out of his home and is probably a sole proprietor. He accepts all major credit cards. He offers a large discount on mini blinds while still promising a three-day delivery. No hours are listed, so he probably works around his clients' schedules. If you do this examination with each of your competitors, you will have a great start in determining a niche that you can fill.

You may be tempted to learn more about the competition by pretending to be a customer interested in their services and asking for their free in-home estimates or by taking up designers' time on the telephone by asking them to tell you all about their services. This is inherently dishonest and certainly disrespectful of their time. You will not want someone to do it to you and, while it may happen occasionally, it does not justify it. When you do open your business, it will be clear to anyone you did this to and you could easily find yourself blackballed. It's a small world and should be seen as a collegial one. It's more honest to pick up the telephone, introduce yourself, and ask if you might take them for lunch to "pick their brain." Seeking a mentor is a much more professional way to go.

That said, if they own a public shop, there is no reason you can't go in and browse, chat briefly with the owner or sales staff, or maybe pick up some brochures. Don't take up too much time because time spent on you is possibly lost sales dollars for them.

Sample Competitor Advertisement

BILL'S HOME EMPORIUM
Mini blinds 70% off   3-day delivery
Vertical blinds   Shutters
Shades   Draperies
Carpet   Wallpaper
Upholstery   Fabrics
FEATURING GRABER PRODUCTS
555-1234
M/C Visa Discover

Other Sources of Information

Another way to get valuable information is to talk to your manufacturers' representatives. They know everyone and have a wealth of knowledge about how your competition is doing and how they do what they do. Amazingly, most representatives will tell you much of what you really need to know without giving up "trade" secrets. You don't want to push someone beyond their comfort level; after all, at this point you have no track record and you're asking the rep to dish on much better and bigger customers. No good rep will be fooled into being too chatty with a newbie.

Sample Competitor Worksheet

Name _____   Phone_____

Address _____   Target Area _____

Focus Product _____   Credit Cards? _____

In-House Installers?_____

Product/ Service	Manufacturers Used	Notes on Discounts Offered

Yet another source of information is installers. If you use a contractor instead of a salaried employee, that contractor will be working for your competition as well. The installer may tell you who's keeping him or her busy and who isn't, and that in turn will tell you how much business the competition is doing.

While all these people are good sources of information, it's important to remember that if they talk to you, they'll also talk to your competition. Keep that in mind because what goes around comes around.

The Bidding and Estimating Process

We'll first discuss putting together your bid or estimate for a product that you are selling to a client. Following this, we'll talk about estimating your design time if you're going to be doing a design plan for the client.

Pricing Your Products

In this type of business you are somewhat in the middle. You are not making the goods yourself—you are buying them from a manufacturer or design center and then reselling them or you are buying some kind of finished goods like fabric and having a workroom manufacture custom window treatments or upholstered furniture. In this chapter we discuss the process of arriving at your selling price. To do this, you first need to understand how to determine your purchase price for product and labor.

Most vendors' prices are nonnegotiable, but some may be and any additional discounts that you can negotiate will only help your bottom line. The size of your discount is the factor that determines how much you will pay for a product and this process varies vendor to vendor. We briefly discuss each of the types of products and how they are priced so that you will be prepared when you set up your accounts.

Hard Line Window Coverings

In the hard window covering industry, you will not work with a wholesale price list but will be assigned a "cost factor," which is a percentage off the retail prices. The discounts vary from business to business, depending on your sales history and, in some cases, which sample programs you have bought into.

Carpet

Carpet companies operate from a wholesale price list versus a retail price list. These prices may be negotiable, but only after you have an established track record of high sales volume. Unless you plan on specializing in carpet, this will probably

**Comparative Chart
for Samples**

TYPE OF PRODUCT	MANUFACTURER	SAMPLE COST	REBATES	FINAL COSTS

not be your best-selling item; it's just too hard to compete with the larger carpet stores. There are many stores that will install carpet for less than you have to pay for the same product. Most of your carpet jobs will come from "complete package" jobs—in other words, jobs where you quote the customer a single price for designing an entire room or house.

Wallpaper

Wallpaper companies very often require that you subscribe to a sample plan. The larger the plan, the bigger your discounts will be. The larger plans are also the most expensive and when you're just starting out in business, it can be hard to justify this cost. In the beginning, you can use a designer showroom or you may be able to share samples with another designer and pool your resources.

The manufacturer discount comparative worksheet given here will help you keep the various manufacturers' discounts straight. You will use this worksheet throughout your time in business because you want to be able to keep track of where your best discounts are coming from.

Product Sales

Putting together a bid or estimate for a single product or an entire kitchen can be complicated and time-consuming. While it's not "hard" per se, there are many pieces and parts that you need to account for and if you miss something and they accept your price, you really cannot go back and increase your quoted price. We've all done it and it's a tough lesson to learn. Based on your market research and knowledge of product pricing, you already should have a good idea what the standard retail prices are for your products and your vendors will be telling you what your purchase price is for that item. The difference between the two is your profit margin. You should have an idea of the profit margin with which you are comfortable and can make a living on. With time and experience, you will learn which products generate the most sales and which you make the most money from. They may or may not be the same. You have already calculated your overhead costs, so now you have to take into consideration the cost of the product, the cost of your time, and the cost of any contract labor.

Make sure that you include all of the following in each of your estimates:

- The cost of the product
- The cost of all labor (e.g., drapery workroom, installations)
- Freight and delivery charges
- Your markup
- Any additional materials or costs

Manufacturer			
Product	Discount	Product	Discount
Product	Discount	Product	Discount
Product	Discount	Product	Discount
Product	Discount	Product	Discount
Manufacturer			
Product	Discount	Product	Discount
Product	Discount	Product	Discount
Product	Discount	Product	Discount
Product	Discount	Product	Discount
Manufacturer			
Product	Discount	Product	Discount
Product	Discount	Product	Discount
Product	Discount	Product	Discount
Product	Discount	Product	Discount
Manufacturer			
Product	Discount	Product	Discount
Product	Discount	Product	Discount
Product	Discount	Product	Discount
Product	Discount	Product	Discount

Figuring Product Costs

Let's go through an example of how you work up a price for a sale of a piece of carpet when working from a wholesale price list. We will get into specific details of how to measure and figure yardage for carpet jobs in chapter 9, but for now imagine that we are bidding a job to carpet 100 yards of a house (when we say yards, we mean square yards). Your vendor will have supplied you with your price lists from which you will know your cost per square yard of the carpet. Now you need to add on labor (installation), padding, and your profit on the carpet. For the purpose of this example, let's price labor at $4 per yard and padding at $3 per yard. (Be sure to check in your own area for the going rates on installation.) Your customers have selected a carpet that is $8.99 per yard at your cost. You have to decide that you are comfortable with a $3-per-yard profit (33 percent) on the carpet and a 25-percent markup on the labor. Your final price to your customer will be $2,074.00 plus tax and delivery, as the following calculations show:

Price of Carpet (*cost plus profit*)	$8.99 + $3 = $11.99 per yard
Price of Labor and Pad (*cost plus markup*)	$7 + 25% = $8.75 per yard
Total Price per Yard	$11.99 + $8.75 = $20.74 per yard
Price for 100 Yards of Carpet	$20.74 x 100 = $2,074.00 (plus tax and delivery)

In this scenario, your total job cost is $1,599 and the client has paid $2,074, resulting in a profit of $475, which is almost 30%. Take a look at your overhead and the time you spent on the job. Is it worth it to you? If not, add another dollar or so per yard to the job if the market will bear it. You may find that a 35-percent profit is more appropriate for your needs. You should keep regular track of your markup percentages and net profits. A tweak here and there can make a big difference to your bottom line. That said, you also need to keep tabs on where your prices are sitting within the marketplace at large. Too low and people may think they are inferior; too high and customers will look elsewhere.

Now let's take a look at how to price a job when you are working with a retail price list and dealer discounts. Let's imagine you are bidding on a bamboo shade and the customer has a window size of 75 by 84 inches. The customer has chosen a bamboo called "Natural." Look at the sample of what a retail price list would look like. The retail price of the Natural bamboo shade is $243. The way you determine that price is to find the width (75 inches) across the top of the price chart and then the length down the side (84 inches), rounding up to the numbers nearest to your measurements. Thus, the price for your 75-by-84-inch blind is the same as an 80-by-95-inch blind: $243.

The retail prices on these price charts are rarely the actual selling prices. Competition in the marketplace, not to mention online resources, has made pricing a little bit like the Wild West: It's every man and woman for himself or herself. That said, sell too low and you'll never make a living and sell too high (unless you have the right clientele) and you won't have too many sales.

A standard sale for a bamboo shade can vary from 20 to 40 percent off. That means you would sell the shade to your customer for between $145.80 (40 percent off) and $194.40 (20 percent off) plus tax and installation.

Retail Price	$243.00
Less 52% discount (cost factor)	− $126.36
Your price	$116.64

Your profit margin on that shade would be between $29.16 and $77.76. Unfortunately, internet retailers who have no brick and mortar overhead costs and have big discounts in place usually cannot be beat when it comes to pricing. For this reason, offering great service and creative design advice is where you can stand out from the big boys on the block. If your state has a sales tax, you will need to add the tax and an installation charge to your price. Later in this chapter you will find an explanation of how to hire a contract laborer and what to pay that person. Sales tax—how to collect and pay it—is also discussed.

The Competitive Bid

As stated earlier, you will be asked to match competitors' prices on a routine basis. You must know how to break down their price to figure out what product the competitor is selling so that you can determine if you can match that price. This happens very often with window covering products, so we'll use those as an example.

Avoid the Deep Discount Temptation

Before discussing matching pricing, here is an important piece of advice: Once you set your price, stick to it. Whether you are primarily product focused or a design consultant, window treatments will probably be the largest portion of your product sales, especially in the beginning, because you don't have to be a large store to gain access to good products and competitive prices. Window treatments are also usually the most needed item in the home for reasons of privacy, light, and temperature control, not to mention aesthetics.

Bamboo Shade Retail Price Chart (Natural)

width	up to 24"	48"	56"	68"	80"	95"	104"
24"	48.00	60.00	80.00	100.00	120.00	150.00	210.00
48"	60.00	75.00	93.00	127.00	149.00	168.00	238.00
56"	89.00	96.00	110.00	139.00	162.00	179.00	249.00
68"	100.00	123.00	136.00	152.00	189.00	210.00	273.00
80"	122.00	140.00	153.00	173.00	199.00	256.00	310.00
95"	138.00	156.00	174.00	198.00	243.00	276.00	353.00
104"	156.00	177.00	190.00	233.00	276.00	299.00	397.00

Many people will start a window covering business and sell the products for a small dollar amount over their cost. These people don't stay in business long, but there are always one or two popping up somewhere. Ignore them.

Of course there will be occasional exceptions to the rule of sticking to your price. You may be doing a large job and the customer asks you to do a small bedroom window at a discounted price. That's okay, because you've probably made a good profit on the rest of the job. Let's say you have a customer you've been working with on designing her entire home. On the last room she fell in love with a fabric that cost $30 a yard over her budget. In a case like that, you might lower the price of the fabric. As a general rule, however, don't give deep discounts. There will always be someone selling window coverings for less than you do. There is a market for that type of business, but I would advise you to stay away from it. You will work twice as hard for half the amount of money as someone who doesn't resort to deep discounts to make a sale. The best thing you can do for your business is to offer great service and customer experience, which can't be done when you're making no money. You can also learn how to upgrade the products you sell, which we will discuss later in this chapter in "Up-Selling." First, we'll discuss how to match a price, product for product.

Matching a Competitor's Price

Let's say you have just given a price for twenty-four high-quality shades in a new home and your estimate is $4,800. You have built up a good rapport with the customer and you have high hopes that you will get the job. Just when you are pulling out the contract for signatures, the customer mentions they have a bid from one of your competitors showing that they've priced the job at $4,000. Then the customer tells you that if you match the competitor's price, you can have the job. If you sold the same product you bid on for $4,800, your profits would instantly be reduced by $800. It's not likely that your competitor has bid the same product that low, unless it's a big box store whose buying power can't be matched. Here's where your product knowledge comes in handy. Manufacturers often sell different grades of products: good, better, and best.

If you come across a bid that is much lower than yours, it is probably based on a lower-grade product. If you have a copy of the competitive bid, it will make the comparison easier because you can then point out the name of the lower-grade blind to your client and adjust your bid appropriately if you wish to. If you don't have a copy of the bid, you will have to try to explain the differences in the product to your customer and then ask him or her to provide you with the detailed bid he or she is referring to. Without that, you cannot match their price without running the risk of losing your shirt.

Estimate versus Bid or Quote?

The main difference between an estimate and a bid or quote is that a bid or quote is your final word. You may give an estimate (a rough price, subject to change) over the phone, but you should give a written quote (a written promise to do the work for a specified amount of money) only after you have measured the house yourself and are confident that you have all of the pertinent information.

Up-Selling

Some people get into the bad habit of selling everything they have to offer at greatly discounted prices. By doing that, you put your business in an unstable position because you have to sell twice as much as someone who doesn't give deep discounts; therefore, when times are slow, your business will be in danger. Rather than selling everything at a deep discount, you can select certain products to be your "loss leader" items that are discounted deeply. A loss leader is a product that is advertised at a high discount to persuade consumers to call you. You can selectively deep discount items without losing your shirt (call it a marketing cost) but if you sold everything at that low of a profit, you wouldn't make enough money to support your business. The counter to the losses incurred by your loss leader products are the products you up-sell. There are better and more expensive products that are not commonly discounted and might be new and special in the eyes of the buyer. If you get to know these products, you can present them to your customer and increase your chances of a larger sale. For instance, if you sold a job of approximately eighteen wood blinds instead of the same number of mini blinds, you would stand to make a couple thousand dollars more on that one job. If you sold hardwood floors instead of carpet, you would also put a few thousand more dollars into your pocket.

Luckily, today's consumers have a better understanding of quality than did those of the past. There are still some people looking for the cheapest blinds or wallpaper, but that's okay—leave those jobs to your competitors. It's your responsibility to educate consumers about the choices they have. It can be a good idea to show samples of the best blind as well as a mid-quality blind, or the best upholstery fabric and the mid-range. If you show the customer the differences in the products and compare the costs, they will usually invest in the better-quality product. Even if they don't, you've still given them a choice. Some sales people will automatically bid on the lowest-priced product because they are afraid that if they try to up-sell, they will lose the job. Actually what happens is that the customer loses faith in them when their product doesn't hold up, and when they are ready to do additional work they will call someone else. That is no way to accumulate repeat business.

Another way to up-sell is to pay attention to the customers' needs. Do they have a sun problem? A mini blind won't keep out the heat, but a solar cellular shade will. Do they have children or pets? Perhaps instead of plain cotton they may wish to try one of the fabulous new indoor/outdoor high-resilience fabrics available today. Too many salespeople are in the habit of parroting back to the client what they say they are looking for and not paying attention to what the customers really need. You must learn to listen to what each customer is telling you. A lot of sales are lost that way because consumers' true needs are not being heard and, therefore, not being met. Pay attention to their needs and you will automatically sell more expensive products.

Sales Tax

We talked about the basics of sales tax in chapter 2. If you live in a sales-tax state, you know you will have to collect the required percentage for your state (and city if applicable) and make monthly or quarterly payments to the government. Some sales-tax states do not require that you charge sales tax on labor. (Be sure to check with your local tax office.) In those cases you would charge tax only on the product that you sell and then add the installation charge after you've added the tax.

Contract Labor

Until you have built up enough business to hire full-time employees, most of your help will be on a contract-labor basis. A person who works as a contract laborer works for many companies and is considered self-employed. For instance, the drapery workroom who fabricates your custom draperies and bedding ensembles will work for many designers and companies. At the end of the year, you will issue individuals a 1099 tax form instead of a W-2 form. You will not take any taxes out of their pay because they will be responsible for them. Some of the other people you will pay as contract labor include carpet layers, wallpaper hangers, drapery workroom laborers, upholsterers, and window covering installers. One of your biggest challenges will be to find a good, reliable contractor for each of these areas. The following method will help you find respected workers.

First, call the various drapery workrooms and set up appointments with them. You can get the names of the workrooms from your drapery manufacturer representative, online, or in the Yellow Pages. There are usually some retailers listed in the "Drapery/Wholesale" section of the Yellow Pages along with the true wholesalers. Skip them; they are just trying to pass off as a wholesaler to the public. You can pick them out by expressions such as "wholesale directly to you" or other slogans directed toward the retail customer. True wholesale workrooms will generally say in their ad that they sell to the trade only. If you are in doubt, call them and pretend to be a retail customer who needs draperies and see whether they agree to bid on the job. Some of the best workrooms don't advertise because they get their business from word of mouth, so be sure to ask around. You will want to interview two or three if possible because your rapport and work styles must be in sync.

Experienced workrooms will likely know who the best installers in the area are and they may be willing to put you in contact with them. They will also have their favorite fabric vendors and will give you recommendations.

Once you've gotten all the information from the people at the drapery workroom, call each of the contacts they gave you and start asking the same questions. When you hear a company or a contract laborer mentioned two or three times, it's reasonably safe to use them for your jobs. You can choose to work with only one workroom or you may find that having good relationships with more than one has its advantages as well. If one workroom is backed up and can't get to your project quickly, you may find the other has an opening in its schedule. You may find that different workrooms have substantially different pricing for the same types of work. This is usually due to experience and the depth of their ability to produce custom and unique work. If you're having standard drapery panels made, you might not need the elite workroom to handle the project because their pricing may be much higher than that of a more "average" workroom. The panels are easy and straightforward and not worth the higher price point. However, you may be designing something more complicated and it's worth paying a higher price to know that the elite workroom will do it perfectly for you. Knowing who is the best vendor for your custom work is essential to delivering a great product to your client and making money in the process.

If you're looking for a carpet installer, ask your sales rep or manufacturer to give you a list of their recommended installers. Call them for their price lists for measuring and installations.

Important Workroom Hint

A good workroom is your essential partner in design. They will verify your yardage and labor estimates before you order the fabric as well as look over your designs and alert you if there are any flaws you should be aware of. Make use of their experience; it can save you from making some very rookie mistakes. Some workrooms will have a selection of drapery and upholstery fabrics that they will sell at their cost plus a reasonable markup. This service comes in handy, for example, when you are looking for an exact shade of yellow and you don't have it in any of your own sample books.

Scheduling Contract Labor

If you are using contract laborers, remember that their time is their own. They are working with several other designers, so you should schedule your installations as far in advance as you can. One way to make planning easier is to hang an erasable board on your wall with the set installations on one side and the tentative installations on the other. If you are using contract labor, it's wise to have backup installers to call in case your main installer has another obligation when you need him or her. As you get busier and start giving the contractor more business, they will begin to put your needs ahead of people who don't give them as much business. Eventually you may find that you are busy enough that you can justify an on-staff installer.

Hiring Your Own Hourly Contractors

One way to reduce installation costs (for any type of installer) may be to hire an employee and train the person to install various products. (Many manufacturers hold installation training seminars that you can attend and send your employees to at no charge.) This only works if you truly have a lot of regular installation work to offer because once the installer is on your regular payroll, you will be paying him whether or not you have any work for him to do. In addition, you will have employment taxes, social security, health coverage, and all the associated costs of having employees.

Payday

Most drapery workrooms and other contractors will require that their fees be paid in full when the product is picked up or, in the case of installers, when they have done their job. If you can, you should try to be at each installation to make sure there are no questions or problems, though this may not be possible or practical if you have a lot of projects going on. If you cannot be at an install, you might require that your installer fill out the job report sheet on page 115. The idea is that the contractor will fill out the sheet and hand it in to you along with his or her invoice. You should never pay on a job without one if you haven't seen the final work in person. (Be sure to let them know this before you hire them.) The sheet will inform you of any problems that occurred on the job and what steps, if any are possible, the installer has taken to correct them. For instance, if a vertical blind is 2 inches too short, has the installer left it in place or taken it down? Did the installer check to be sure he or she didn't accidentally install the wrong blind in the wrong window and there is another slightly smaller window that has a too-long shade installed? This is all part of what processes and procedures you have in place and training your contractors to do things as you wish they are done. Many interior designers request that the client pay the installer directly versus running it through the business. If you aren't taking a markup on the installer's fee, then you are actually doing more work without compensation. Even if you are on site, you can require the client to pay directly. If you are not on site, you have to be sure that you truly trust your installers to be able to troubleshoot any problems professionally and that they are representing your brand well.

Interior Design Consulting Fees

We've spent a lot of time discussing how to price standard products used in the business. There are many more products and manufacturers to contend with such as tile, cabinetry, wood flooring, electronics—the list is really endless, but the process is generally the same. But if your business focus is on interior design consulting, you will also need to figure out how to charge for your services of creating a design plan, which may include space planning, lighting plans, sourcing fabrics, furnishings and finishes, procurement, and installation. The complicating factor here is that there is no set industry standard. One of the hardest things to do is to set a value on our own work, especially when we're new in business. Insecurity can be our worst enemy in this regard. When we're selling a product, it's a tangible thing with real costs associated with the sales price. Even if you're asked for a discount, it's a discount on an inanimate object, not on you yourself. And that's what happens when we come to putting a price on our own talent, creativity and the intangible that is our "advice." Some clients truly value and admire our talents, but many others don't understand the true value of our knowledge, experience, and creative energy. As with product pricing, you may be tempted to discount yourself, but you will never make money doing so and you are only hurting your brand. Of course, as a new designer in business, you are not going to start at a top rate, but you shouldn't start too low either. Our hourly rate is really just the starting point, but it's the most important number to come up with. First, you need to know what is standard in your area. Naturally, designers in New York City with high rents and costs of living will charge a higher hourly rate than someone in a more rural area. Start by viewing the websites of local designers to see if they share their pricing structures. Larger firms will have different fees for the principal designers and owners than what they charge per hour for a junior or associate designer. As new designer, especially if you don't have a lot of formal design training or experience, you will bill closer to the junior associate rate of a large firm. Doing this kind of research may or may not reveal to you exact pricing, but you will hopefully get an idea of the range. You might also call up an established designer and simply ask him or her what the going rate is in the area. True professionals won't have a problem discussing it in broad terms; they may or may not share their own fees, but they might give you a range.

Coming at it from another angle, you should have an idea how much money you need to be earning to support your lifestyle. If you need (not want, but need) to bring in a gross income of $50,000 then divide that number by fifty weeks (leave yourself two weeks for vacation) and you will need to earn $1,000 a week, which is $25 per hour if your week has forty billable hours. But it rarely will nor would you want it to if you're a one-person shop because you will be working at least another twenty hours, probably more, on unbillable tasks such as bookkeeping, marketing, and keeping up on product lines. Double the hourly rate to $50 and you will need to bill twenty hours a week—which may not sound difficult, but can be, especially for a start-up.

> Broadly, interior design hourly rates range from $75 for a new designer to up to $200 for an established designer and well more for superstar celebrity designers.
>
> But your hourly rate is just a guideline.

There are four standard ways that designers charge for their time.

Hourly Rate with a Markup on Any Product Sold

With the hourly rate with markup method, you will put an estimate on how many hours you expect to work on the project and take a markup on any products you sell. While it seems simple, few clients will want an open-ended arrangement and will need you to put a clear estimate on the number of hours you anticipate a job will take. You will take a deposit against your estimated total and keep track of every minute you spend on that project, which is not easy if you're bounding from client to client. The potential upside is that if the project expands from the initial scope of work, you can keep charging for more hours. The downside, however, is that the more experience you gain, the less time (therefore fewer billable hours) you will be spending on your jobs. The more you know, the less you earn, which is certainly the opposite of where you want to be headed. In addition to the design rate, you will also be earning a percentage on the products you sell. The previous section of this chapter goes into great detail about how to mark up products and the method is the same here. You may not necessarily take as large a markup because you're earning a design fee, but that's entirely up to you and what the market will bear.

Hourly Rate with No Markup on Products

Many designers have chosen to be completely transparent and charge a higher hourly design rate and pass along all product discounts direct to their clients. This method may appeal to the client who is looking for "insider deals" but there are drawbacks. You have to be able to justify a higher hourly rate, which your newbie status may not support. And if you end up having to eat the cost of a mismeasure or undercharge (perhaps you forgot to include the price of the installer in the quote for window treatments) you are going to be taking that loss off the top of your hourly fees as you will not have product cushion to fall back on. But if your hourly rate is significant enough, it may work for you.

Flat Fee, No Markup

More and more, designers are going toward the flat-fee method of billing for a project. Historically, designers charged a smaller fee, or hourly rate, and based much of their income on product sales. However, the discounted online availability of nearly any product we sell, including many traditionally "trade-only" goods, has drastically reduced our income on product sales. Many clients are shopping on their own and finding suitable alternatives, or the exact products, we are specifying. It can be enormously frustrating to have created a beautiful plan and counted on the income you will earn on your markups only to have the client find some or all of it at a better price. The flat-fee method means that you will have come up with a fee that pays you well for your design expertise—which is the real "gold" of what you're selling—and if the client wants to go elsewhere for the product, you aren't losing income. You can specify products from retail stores or pass along your designer discounts. However, charging no markups does leave you short if there are problems with products you do sell. And there are always problems.

Flat Fee with Markup

As with the previous method, you will be charging a fee that is sufficient for the talent and expertise you bring to the project. You will clearly define the scope of the project and not let it expand without a revision of the contract and your fee. Should the client wish you to do the purchasing, or there are products the client cannot purchase for himself or herself, you will charge a separate "buyer's" fee which is usually a percentage on top of your product cost. This fee, which may range anywhere from 10 to 35 percent, is to pay you for your time spent ordering, tracking, receiving, and installing the product. Don't underestimate the time this process takes. If there are problems with the product, you will be dealing with all of that. If clients wish to purchase something themselves, then you take no responsibility and should not spend any time dealing with it. In the case that clients ask for your help if there's a problem, you can advise them of your hourly rate and charge by the hour to help them out. Please note that this buyer's fee is added to retail purchases as well. Some clients may balk at this, but adding 35 percent onto a $500 coffee table from a retail chain is only $175 for you. For this, you could spend a couple of hours of time if all goes well, or you might spend many hours correcting problems that might arise. If the client still has problems, then they can simply do the buying themselves.

There are other methods of billing as well.

- Some designers only charge a markup on the products they sell and forgo a design fee, but this is the fast track to bankruptcy if you actually need to be earning a living—unless your clientele is so upscale that you're regularly selling hundreds of thousands of dollars of goods on each project.

- Some designers charge a per-square-foot pricing on the assumption that a larger house is a bigger job than a smaller house.

- Projects that have a construction component may be billed at a percentage of the total project budget, but this type of project is generally out of the scope of this book.

As you can see, it's not easy to figure out the billing process that works best for you. The most important thing is to keep on top of your earnings and regularly analyze your procedures to be sure that you are billing your clients an appropriate amount for time and talent you are devoting to their project. With experience, you will learn where your "sweet spot" profit margin on each job should be. It could be 30 percent or 45 percent. Once you have a good feel for this profit percentage, you will know upon hearing a client's desired budget if the job is right for you because you will know approximately how much you can expect to earn. Not all clients are right for us and we're not right for every client. It's always a two-way street and the quicker we realize which direction we're going in, the better for all.

An Inspirational Word

Don't be discouraged if after reading this far you don't feel like an expert. If you read this book and do all of the exercises, you will be well prepared for your first appointment, though nothing beats the knowledge you will gain from just going out there and learning on the job. In the next chapter you will learn more about the in-home estimate. Chapter 9 delves into product knowledge and gives you specifics on measuring and figuring yardage. That chapter has some worksheets for you to practice with before actually going on an appointment.

Installer Job Critique Sheet

SM_____ Date _____

Address _____

Product installed _____

Notes (If problems, include room or window location and nature of problem.)

_____

_____

_____

_____

Steps taken to correct problems

_____

_____

_____

_____

Installer's Name _____ Cust. Pd? _____

Installer's Signature _____

Amount of Invoice _____

(Attach copy)

08

Thus far everything in this book has prepared you for the appointment. You've set up your business legally, you've run your figures and prepared your business plan, and you know how much overhead you have and how much business you need to do to sustain your business. You have met with the various manufacturers' reps and showrooms and have decided which companies you are going to do business with. You've negotiated for the best sample prices and discounts possible, you have set up all of your files and created a contract format, and you've finally started to advertise. You handled your first estimate call aptly and turned it into an appointment. Right now, you're probably feeling a little nervous. It's time to take a look at what happens at this initial in-home meeting. It's important that you take the lead from the beginning and stay in control throughout the appointment because that will better your chances for a sale. To do this you'll need to know what to expect and how to handle various situations that may come up.

The Appointment

Your work begins well before you walk through the door of your prospective client's home.

Before the Appointment

The client prospect will have either called you or emailed you, depending on how they heard about you. Generally it's best to communicate with prospects in the manner that they wish to communicate. For instance, if they want to email because they have a busy schedule, it's wise to understand this. However, there is nothing like a real conversation when you want to truly understand who the person is and what their needs are. So if they contact you by email but include their phone number, then pick up the phone and call them. If they don't include their telephone number, email them back and suggest a phone conversation. When you set up the appointment over the phone, it's obvious that you will want to ask the customer what type of work he or she is interested in doing. Once you find out the type of product or services the customer is looking for, you can ask more specific questions as outlined at the end of chapter 6. This will help you know what samples to take with you on the appointment. It may be tempting, but don't take too many samples because that tends to confuse the customer. It's your job to determine what products will best serve the customer's needs. For instance, if the customer is interested in Plantation shutters, you should take samples from your preferred manufacturer but keep a different one in the car as a backup. Use it if the customer can't find anything she or he likes in the first sample book. The same idea applies to any product you are selling. If it's a carpet appointment and you have already established that the customer wants a Berber, carry in three different Berber styles from a high, middle, and low price range. Keep a few more Berber samples in the car in case the customer doesn't find anything pleasing in the ones you carry in. While it may be tempting to carry in lots of samples to demonstrate that you carry lots of product and have deep product knowledge, one of the reasons homeowners want in-home service (versus going to a big box store) is so that their choices are culled down to the best options.

Make sure you have the appropriate price lists for every product you take with you. You should also have price lists for all the other products that you sell, because if something comes up that you hadn't expected, you will need to give the customer an estimate. Besides your samples, you will also want to take along a tape measure, camera, calculator, pens and pencils, appointment book, notebook, graph paper, and sample contracts or estimate sheets. Use the notebook to record the measurements and the graph paper to draw the room diagram for carpet or the design of the window. If it's a fairly straightforward product sale, you should be able to give them all pricing and options details right on the spot, write up the order, and seal the deal. If something is more complicated, or if you will be working on a design plan for a room or the whole house, you will be more likely to want to gather all the information you can and put together your pricing and contract details in the office to be presented at a followup meeting. Walking away from the first meeting without a signed order and deposit may seem counterintuitive, but you never want to appear rushed or make mistakes that you have to eat down the road. Just be sure to schedule the followup within a day or so.

It's helpful to get specific directions to the customer's house or office while you are on the phone. If you have GPS, you might ask if the house is easily findable in this manner. New subdivisions may not be. New homeowners may not really know how to direct someone to their house yet from all directions, so you may need to figure it out yourself. If you don't have GPS (and you really should), keep a good street map with you. It's important to remember that you must be on time to your appointments—always. Even if the client gave you bad directions, you really don't want to be blaming them as your excuse for being late. First impressions are the key to successful sales, and you won't make a good one by being late.

Additional tips on making a good first impression:

- Don't be late, but never be early either. If you arrive early, drive up the street, park and relax for a few minutes, freshen your makeup or comb your hair.

- Avoid drinking beverages (water is okay) or eating in the car en route to an appointment, or keep a change of clothes handy. Stains don't make the best first impression.

- Remove sunglasses before the door is answered and wipe your hands in the event they are clammy.

- It's okay to bring a small bottle of water in your bag if you feel you need it (e.g., you get dry mouth from nerves or you have a small cough) but don't carry in any other beverage. A nice homeowner (and someone you wish to work with) will offer you something to drink once you're settled.

Arriving at the Appointment

After you arrive on time and introduce yourself, start building a rapport with the customer. Some homeowners will be speaking to more than one designer or vendor, so you will want to leave a good lasting impression with them. There is an old saying: "People buy from people they like" and most people will pay more money to work with someone they trust. Ideally, you want both. You should strive to make customers feel comfortable with you and let them know that you are looking out for their best interests. One of the easiest ways to do that is by building a rapport with them. Do this by first talking about small things; maybe they have the same color scheme as you do, or perhaps they have a collection of sailboats that interest you. In some cases you may come across prospects who aren't interested in small talk, so pay attention to their physical and verbal cues and move along to the job at hand quickly. For them, this show of respect for their time may be rapport building in and of itself.

After you have established a satisfactory rapport, you should ask for a tour of the room or rooms that the customer intends to work on. Take a mental inventory of the styles and colors in each room, noting any additional suggestions that you can mention later. For instance, if the customer wants to change the color of the draperies in the study, be sure to take note or photos of the other furnishings in the room. If the new fabric they like doesn't match what else is in the space, you may have a larger project in the offing. The same principle applies to bedrooms; does the homeowner realize that you can also provide bedspreads, wallpaper, and carpet to go with the new draperies?

Next, you should sit down with your client and look at the sample books to determine what textures and colors appeal to her or him. The client may have already decided on the desired colors. In that case you should pinpoint the textures and styles the client is drawn to. For instance, some people are drawn to the shiny, smooth texture of chintz fabric whereas others are drawn to the rough look and feel of a textured linen. Many people have a hard time verbalizing their preferences, so ask them to look through a few magazines or your portfolio and point out which styles they like. From your phone conversation you probably have determined the budget for the project. Confirm this now and you can steer your customer toward the products that will fit into their budget while keeping their specific needs in mind. Your desired goal for this portion of the sale is to determine your client's design plans, color and style preferences, and intended budget.

Dealing with the client budget is one of the most important aspects of the sales process, but not because you are trying to get them to spend more than they want to. Some prospects will have no idea how much things cost and when asked what their budget is will say that they don't know or will offer up a budget amount that is completely unreasonable for the work they want accomplished. Others are afraid that if they give you a dollar amount, you will automatically exceed it. But, for all those obstacles, it's essential that you get them to agree to a dollar amount. Of course, for clear-cut product sales, you will be quickly able to quote them different price points based on your good-better-best product lines and show them the difference between the different levels. For larger product installations and interior decorating projects you probably won't be able to quote final pricing in the first meeting and so getting them to disclose what they are willing to spend is very important. If you come across resistance, you need to carefully explain that you need to know the budget so you know how to offer them the best selections for their money. For instance, will you be shopping in a retail store for them or going the full-on custom and trade-only route? Do they expect the best money can buy or are they looking for budget items? Perhaps it's a mix. You can always help them understand their budget options by assigning rough dollar amounts to specific items in a space. This is where a deep knowledge of pricing comes in handy. For instance, perhaps they are looking for you to do window treatments for an entire house (thirty-five windows let's say) and it's a mix of hard treatments and soft fabric ones. You can suggest that a "good" price level is about $500 on average per window (some may be more, some less) for product and installation, "better" is $1,000, and "best" is $1,500. So, by this method, you are advising them that their "good" range is $17,500, the "better" is $35,000, and the "best" is $52,500. They will quickly tell you which range they are in. Similarly, if you are estimating a budget to decorate a living room and the client wants to spend $10,000, you can quickly help the client realize that this is probably not a big enough budget. You can outline that a moderately priced rug of decent quality is at least $1,500, a sofa is $2,500, six windows $3,000 to $6,000, and coffee and side tables are going to be $1,000 to $2,500. Plus you'll need lamps, art, and accessories. By breaking it down, you are helping the client understand the importance of upfront budgeting. A final note: never let a client tell you that he or she has no budget and is open to seeing what you come up with. If you turn up with a $10,000 coffee table recommendation, you are likely to quickly hear about budget limits after all and you will most certainly have wasted your time.

Measuring

We will discuss the actual process for measuring the specific products in chapter 9, but for now we will discuss the general rules. Remember that it's vital to be able to concentrate while you measure. While it seems pretty straightforward, you don't want to accidentally read 70 inches as 7 feet. Surprisingly, the biggest threat to your concentration is your customer. Most people don't understand the concentration level needed to think a job through, and so many of them will follow you around and talk while you are trying to measure. As you will learn in chapter 9, a mistake of an eighth of an inch can result in a product that doesn't fit. The easiest thing to do is simply be honest with your client and tell them that it is more accurate and will go quicker if you are left to your own. Most will understand this and will give you space to do your job. But not all clients will truly get this and will still follow you around chatting. In these cases, keep the customer occupied with something else while you measure. For instance, you might keep your customer occupied by assigning a task such as going through magazines, websites, or sample books to highlight items that speak to them. This strategy will not only allow you to measure without interruption, you will also be gaining excellent input from the client about what he or she likes, or even doesn't like.

Pricing

There are two schools of thought on when it's best to make your bid. Some designers like to give the client a price during the first appointment because they think it will increase the chance for a sale. They figure that the client is excited about everything you've shown and to leave without quoting a price will break the momentum and give the client time to reconsider. On the other hand, a large project could take too much time to estimate—hours in some cases—or you don't have all the information you need at hand. It's really quite rare for a big job to give any kind of accurate pricing on the spot. If you're a consulting designer, you should have already asked for a deposit against your time and the rest will follow.

The first school of thought is a strong one, and it's backed by experience. The chance of closing the sale does go up considerably if you can present the bid to the client during the first appointment. If necessary, you could tell the customer that you need about twenty minutes of quiet time to work up the numbers. Most people are happy to oblige and will leave you alone, but some people won't stop talking and will make it impossible to concentrate. In those situations you will have no choice but to tell them that you will call later that day with a bid.

That being said, beginners needn't jump in and attempt to give bids on the first few appointments. Wait until you feel comfortable enough with your products and pricing structures. Spend time practicing your estimating skills and becoming comfortable measuring many different types of spaces.

One thing you will have to be wary of is giving your measurements to the customer. Some customers will try to take advantage of the free in-home estimate. They think that you will come measure their windows and then hand them the measurements or tell them how many rolls of wallpaper and border that they need at the end of the appointment. Then they will go to a home design store armed with your hard-earned measurements and purchase the products off the rack. One way to avoid this situation is to charge for the measurements. If a customer insists on having the measurements, simply tell him or her that you will be happy to sell them for $50 (or whatever you think your time was worth). Let the customer know that if he or she buys from you, the amount will be deducted from your bill. This policy might make some customers angry, but it's the only way you can ensure that your time is not being wasted. Remember, you promised a free in-home estimate for your products and services, not a free measuring job.

The Close

The close is obviously the most important step in selling the job. Show your client the bid and explain that the price includes labor, materials, installation, and tax.

Don't give a breakdown of the price unless clients ask for it because that will do one of two things: It will make it easier for clients to shop around and compare your prices, or it may just confuse them.

If the customer decides to compare your bid with the competition, it will be easy for them to beat the bid by showing a less expensive product. If it's a drapery job that they are comparing, they will know from your breakdown that you are charging $50 per yard for the fabric, $150 per width for labor, and $6 per foot for installation, so all they have to do is offer a lower price for the fabric, or show cheaper goods, to beat your pricing. The same applies to all of your products. You want to make it as difficult as possible for your competitor to break down your bid.

When a customer buys a product, he or she usually thinks of it in terms of a finished product. If you break down a carpet bid and show the individual prices for the carpet, padding, tack strips, installation, and disposal of the old carpet, you are only asking for trouble. The customer will see all the different prices and feel as though it's costing more than if you had just given one figure.

During your presentation of the quote, take note of your client's expression. If the client's face registers a shocked look, she or he has probably not priced custom products before and you have not sufficiently explored their ideas about budgets in the "getting to know you" phase of your meeting. Explain, perhaps for a second time, the quality that they will be getting for the money. Ask for the client's thoughts. If they feel that the price is a little out of range, make alternative suggestions to bring down the price but never reduce your markup and profit to fit their budget. If they don't want to spend at a certain level, then offer them a lower-priced product or less service. But if the client is nodding approvingly throughout the presentation, that is your cue to pull out the contract and ask for the deposit.

Sales 101

Unfortunately, a lot of designers believe that if they are good with space and have a flair for design, jobs will automatically fall into their lap. Not true. You must be good at sales as well to be successful in this business. Take some time to read up on sales techniques or attend a class, and in the meantime, follow these basic rules.

- Assume that you already have the sale. Your attitude will come across as you interact with the client; make sure that it's a confident one. From the moment you walk in the door until the time you pull out the contract, assume that you are there to write up the order.

- Make sure that you are talking to the decision maker. It's very frustrating to spend a couple of hours with a client selling the design of a room only to hear the words, "I'll have to discuss it with my husband," or "I'll have to talk it over with my wife." It's a good idea to schedule the appointment when both the husband and the wife will be at home if it takes both of them to make a decision.

- Sell the features and benefits of a product instead of the product itself. As the saying goes "Sell the sizzle, not the steak." If you relate the fact that hardwood floors will increase the value of a home, it will mean more to your clients than simply pointing out how beautiful wood floors are (they already know that).

- Sell your company, but don't trash your competition. A red flag goes up for many consumers when they hear a salesperson criticizing a competitor. People who feel the need to denigrate their competition are probably trying to overcome some of their own shortcomings. Such behavior is viewed as unprofessional and will usually create negative feelings.

You will face many customer objections in the course of an appointment. It's your job as the designer to listen to the objections and either counter them or find another product that will suit their needs. After you have handled all the objections your customer has brought up, attempt a trial close. The purpose of a trial close is to tell you whether or not you're on the right track with the sale. The following dialogues demonstrate this technique, first with a window covering sale and then with a carpet sale.

> CUSTOMER: I love the beautiful wood look of the shutters you've shown me for my windows, but the price is way over my budget. I guess I'll have to wait until I can save enough money. Thank you for your time.

> YOU: Mrs. Jones, did you realize that my company accepts all major credit cards if that might make it easier for you?

> CUSTOMER: Yes I did, but my husband and I never use credit. We feel that if we can't afford it, we don't really need it.

> YOU: That's a smart way to live, Mrs. Jones. Tell me, how much were you expecting to pay for the shutters?

> CUSTOMER: About half of what you've just quoted me.

YOU: I see. Most people don't realize how much custom shutters cost. However, may I show you some wood blind alternatives that may work well for you? Did you realize that wood blinds are available in two- and three-inch slats and would give you the same beautiful wood look as the shutters? The price of wood blinds is beautiful, too—they run about half the price of shutters!

CUSTOMER: I didn't realize that. Do you have a sample you can show me?

YOU: Absolutely. I'll get them out of the car and I can show you photos of how these look installed.

If your customer answers yes to that question, you have successfully overcome all of her objections. If she says no, you'll have to keep digging to find out what her real objection is. Then you will have to overcome that and try to close her again. Now let's suppose Mrs. Jones wants carpet.

CUSTOMER: I like the color and style of the carpet, but I'm afraid that the light color will show stains.

YOU: Mrs. Jones, you have selected a carpet that gives you a ten-year warranty for stain protection. The carpet is a blend of Olefin and Nylon; these fibers are extremely stain-resistant. The color will achieve the light and airy look you want for the resale value. You get it all in this carpet: style, color, and excellent stain protection. Does this satisfy your concerns?

CUSTOMER: But what about installation? How can I be sure that it will be done right?

YOU: I use a carpet installer who has been in the business for fifteen years. I'd be happy to give you the names and phone numbers of a few of my clients as referrals.

CUSTOMER: That would be great. I know it would put my husband's mind at ease. Do you take credit cards or offer any kind of financing?

YOU: We don't offer private financing, unfortunately, but definitely accept all major credit cards for your convenience.

CUSTOMER: That sounds like what we need.

YOU: Great! Shall we write up the order?

If you're selling your design consulting services, you may hear the following objection:

CUSTOMER: I would love to have you help me with my living room, but your proposed fee is much higher than I was anticipating. We don't have an enormous budget for this, after all, and we're already buying so much.

YOU: Mrs. Jones, I do understand that things can add up quickly. This is a typical project that I handle and you have commented how much you love my portfolio of work. This fee is typical for such a project. As we discussed, you wanted several floor plan options so you could decide the furniture layout you like best, you wanted me to source all the furniture, window treatments, fabrics, lighting and art and show you several options for each. You are also interested in my company handling all the purchasing, receiving and installations for you. I do believe my price is fair for the amount of work involved. Does this answer your concerns?

CUSTOMER: I don't know, it's still so much money. You are so talented, I would love to use you. I've been telling my neighbors all about our meeting.

YOU: Okay, I appreciate that. I can't reduce my fee for all the work we've discussed, but I could reduce the number of options I show you, to say two, and you could handle all the retail store purchases. I think for that, I could take 25% off the price. Is that helpful to you?

At this point, the client will have played his or her hand and either be willing to pay a reduced fee for reduced services, or you may have to walk away. The fact is, not everyone is going to be a good client and there have been some major red-flags in the above exchange that you should have noted. First, the client is putting more emphasis on what she is paying for the goods and not enough on the designer, even though she wants the services of a designer. Second, she is trying to flatter you into relenting on your price. And third, she has subtly suggested that if you work for her, on her terms, there will be more work coming from neighbors.

Stick to your guns. If you can't overcome the objections, walk away and don't waste any more of your time. The reality is, if you reject them, versus them rejecting you, they may have a change of heart about their budget objections.

Before You Leave

Once you have a signed contract in hand, make sure you have recorded all the measurements, taken lots of photos, and have gathered all details pertinent to the sale such as fabric names and colors, future meeting or install dates, and any special items relating to the job. It would be slightly embarrassing to have to go back later and remeasure or reconfirm a fabric choice—though don't hesitate to do so if you need to. Never, ever make a guess. The client will appreciate your thoroughness in the long run. Write down all this information on the contract, being as specific as you can. Also write down the total selling price and note how much deposit was paid. Ask your customer to sign the contract. Once the paperwork has been taken care of, confirm any followup the customer can expect from you, leave your card, and leave on a happy and positive note. Customers want to know you're excited and thankful for their trust.

One of the most commonly heard complaints about designers is lack of follow-through. Call your client within a day or two and confirm your next meeting or estimated delivery date. Keep in regular contact as the project moves forward and return any calls or emails within 24 hours. Some design firms have a set day each week where they call or email all their current customers with a quick update on where their project is. It may seem like a big effort, but this little bit of goodwill goes a long way. Remember, you are always wooing your client and keeping top of mind—they are your best source for referrals to new clients.

Three-Day Right of Rescission

In most states there is a law that gives customers the right to cancel any order that was sold to them in their home within three days. This law will apply to you. Contact your state Attorney General's office to learn how this law applies to your design business. If you wait the three days before you order, that will add three days to your delivery time, so plan accordingly if you've promised quick turnaround. If you don't wait the three days and order the product, you are taking a chance. Let's say that a customer ordered Roman shades for her entire house and needed them immediately. You didn't wait three days before ordering the fabric, and the customer called you on the second day and canceled the order. If the fabric was in stock and you have an open account, your supplier will have already cut and shipped the goods. Unless it is defective, cut fabric is nonreturnable. In your desire to please a customer and close a deal, don't promise more than you can deliver or risk your own bank account. If a client is pushing for an unreasonable turnaround time, you can either get the client to understand what is a reasonable time frame, or you may have to walk away.

If They Didn't Buy at the Appointment

You've done your best. You showed them beautiful products that complement the room and they appeared interested, nodding their heads throughout the presentation. When you handed them the estimate, they thanked you for your time. You explained to them that you will always be on top of their project and you accept credit cards, but they remained vague. They said they would call you and walked you to the door. As you load up your car, you are wondering: "Is it me?"

You will ponder this type of situation many times in your career. Believe it or not, some people will just use you to get ideas; some don't realize how expensive custom products are. Some people may not have enough money and have poor credit. Others are just bored, and a free in-home estimate sounds like a fun way to spend an afternoon. The most probable explanation is that these customers are getting more than one bid. In that case you should make sure you stand out.

You should contact the people with a follow-up call one to two days after the appointment. If they told you they needed to talk it over, ask if they have had time to make any decisions. If they are still vague, send them a letter briefly outlining the project you discussed and confirm the price. State in your letter that you would enjoy working with them. Inject a personal note: something that you discussed during the appointment.

There will be times when you think you've lost a bid, only to receive an order from that person a few months later. Some people are planners; they want to get an idea of the cost and then save for it or think about it for a while. Something could happen in their lives that pushes their plans out six months or more and you won't know. They might hire someone else, later regret it, and come back to you down the road to either fix what went wrong or work on another room or home. In any case, if you use the follow-up methods we've talked about, you will increase your odds of being the person that they call back to do the work. It would be unrealistic to expect to win every job, but if you portray a professional image, are prepared, and follow up your bids accordingly, you will be one step ahead of the competition.

After the Sale

Now that you've sold the job, there's more work to be done. The first thing you will want to do (especially in the beginning) is have your installer or workroom check your material estimates. If you have sold an upholstery job, take your photos and detailed measurements to the upholsterer and have them double-check your yardage estimate before you order the fabric. If you sold draperies, have your drapery workroom check your yardage by showing them your measurements. The same applies to carpet and wallpaper. If you're unsure of your skills at measuring and estimating at first, you may want to check with your contractors before a particularly tricky job is fully estimated. It's better to be safe than sorry and while on-the-spot pricing is a great thing to be able to offer, it will cost you more in the long run if you underestimate and have to eat the extra costs.

Once you have confirmed the amount of material needed, your next step will be to order it. Depending on your vendor's options, you will be ordering by phone, email, online, or fax. It's easy to get in the habit of ordering by phone because it's faster, but you may not know if they have taken the order properly until the wrong thing comes in. Some companies still provide you with ordering forms that can be faxed directly to them and many have now moved this to an online system. Either way you will have the order in black and white and will hopefully receive a confirmation notice back. Here is a sample order for a shade. (Examples of order forms and information requirements for all products will be explained in chapter 9.)

Filing System for Orders

You will need to have a progress system for ongoing orders so that you can check on them as they progress. You will need to be able to determine if a product that you've ordered is running late or simply hasn't shown up. An easy system is to use an expandable file system set up with dates. Mark the tabs as week 1, 2, 3, and 4. When you place an order, you will always be given a projected delivery date. If it's a short turnaround delivery, mark your calendar a couple of days before the due date and pull your paperwork to be ready to either receive the goods or check that the delivery is still on track. If the item is on back order, you will want to regularly check

Quantity	I/S	Width	Length	Controls	Stack	Valance	Style	Color	Price
1	o/s	75	84	left	left	yes	hop	acorn	350

if the backorder date is still in effect or has it been pushed out. Most reputable vendors will automatically notify you of delays, but keep on top of them anyway. Part of our job is to manage the expectations of our clients. If we promise them a delivery by a certain date, you don't want to be giving them bad news the day before they expected delivery. Over time, you will learn which vendors are the most reliable and which need more oversight.

Timelines

Designers can get very busy and forget to order one or two items for a job. It would be embarrassing to have to tell a customer that the reason his order didn't get installed as scheduled is because you forgot to order it. This potential problem can be avoided by completing a timeline, or product ordered form, for each job you get. Place it in the file folder and keep that file in your in basket on your desk. Follow the rule that the file stays in the basket until all the products have been ordered. If you are doing a drapery job, your form would look something like the sample timeline on page 132. The most important thing is to develop a clear set of procedures and follow them to the letter on each and every project. If you have an assistant, train him or her to follow your procedures as well. The more systematic your processes, the fewer mistakes will happen. All that said, if you do make a mistake, or forget to place an order, be upfront with your client that there has been a delay and you will need to reschedule. You don't need to share all the gory details, but you do need to respect that they may be an inconvenience and acknowledge that. The longer the delay, the more you may have to offer to make up for it. Under no circumstances should a mistake on your part (or on your vendor's part) cost your client money.

The Installation

It's crucial that the installation of the product goes well. There are a couple of things you can do to ensure that everything runs smoothly.

First, give the installer specific instructions. This may include drawings, a numbering system so window treatments are installed in the correct windows, and so on. Whatever information you think is needed, he or she should know. It's always best to be at installations if possible, especially for window treatments, but if you cannot be there, your written instructions need to guide the process. Never leave it up to an installer to have to wing it or make assumptions; it's not fair to the installer or to your client.

It would also be beneficial to set up a measuring system with your installers. For instance, if you always measure a house from left to right (facing the front of the house), your installer will know that bedroom number 3 means the third bedroom from the left.

If you are not at an installation, make sure the installer knows what to do if anything goes wrong on the job. Most importantly, the installer should keep quiet about the problem and call you immediately to discuss it. There is nothing worse than an installer who panics on the job and makes the customer lose confidence in you and your work. A good installer will make a complicated or problem-ridden installation look like a breeze, whereas a bad installer will stop at the simplest of obstacles and announce that there are problems and the customer should call you to fix them. Finally, any contractor that you allow into your client's home should understand that they are there working for you and should not get too chummy with the client. If the client starts asking them questions about choices they made with you, they are to simply say that the client needs to discuss that directly with you. Some clients, especially nervous ones, will ask everyone they speak with what they think of their design plans. Giving in to this neurosis only means trouble for you as the designer.

To Go or Not to Go

Once your business starts to take off, you will have to make some hard choices regarding your time. In the beginning you will have time to go to all of your installations to check on the progress of the job. Once you start to get busier, your time will be stretched in many different directions. Your absence at the installation can create a problem with some customers, so you will have to learn how to prioritize which jobs and clients require more hands-on attention and which you can leave to your trusted installers. Some of your customers will request that you be there while others won't care as long as the outcome of the job is good. Generally, the more specialized installations require your presence. For instance, if the installation involves a wood floor with an inlaid pattern, you should definitely be at the installation to direct the installer with specific instructions. It's not always necessary that you stay through the entire installation, but at the minimum make an appearance at the larger ones.

Managing Your Sales

It's easy to become overwhelmed in the home-based interior design business because you will be responsible not only for achieving your self-imposed income goals, but you will also be responsible for the designs, specifications, ordering, and all the little details that lead up to final installation. It's wise to start by setting small, attainable goals in the beginning. Then take those goals and create a plan that will allow you to accomplish them. If your goal is to have three appointments per day, and each appointment lasts approximately two hours, your day is already up to six hours. Add in time for the bookkeeping (one hour) and time for figuring bids and ordering products (three hours), plus marketing and networking, and your day is very long indeed. If that's too much, cut down your number of appointments and plan on marketing higher-end products so each sale will bring in more income. Your goals will change over time as you become more confident. You will also start to establish a selling pattern. If you know that your average sale is $2,000 or $10,000, you will have no problem setting your sales goals.

Next you will need to work on your time management. You will find your to do list to be your most important "go-to" document. At the end of each day, make note of what you accomplished and move the unfinished business to your list, or calendar, for the next day. Start the morning by finishing that list before you do anything else. Set your appointments so that you have either the morning or the afternoon open to take care of paperwork. You may find it necessary to ignore email or telephone calls to keep on top of your to-do lists. Over time, you will learn what works best for you.

Be sure not to set your appointments too close together or you'll spend your time apologizing for arriving late. Allow enough time to do all that you need to do without rushing the client. Simple sales from your sample books may go very quickly, but larger design projects with lots of custom window treatments,

Date of order:

_____

Customer:

_____

Products sold:

Orders

Product	Date Ordered	Est. Delivery Date
Fabric		
Lining		
Tassels		
Hardware		
Work order to workroom		
Installation scheduled		

upholstery, paint colors, and more will take well more than one meeting to finalize the whole design plan.

Another way you can make the best use of your time is to organize your price sheets and formula guides into a sales manual. The next chapter will show you how to put yours together.

09

Product Overview

You now have enough basic knowledge of the design business and how it works to start studying the specifics of the products that you will be working with. Remember, it's always important to present yourself as a professional, and professionals know their products. Over time you will gain more and more knowledge of the products as you work with them, but in the meantime you must be as well-equipped as possible.

This chapter is designed in a way that is most conducive to learning. It's important to know the basics of the products, but it's not necessary to memorize each of the many formulas and charts. It is, however, important to know where to look for the information. You will put together your sales manual in this chapter, and that will serve as a reference guide for when you are on appointments. You will know exactly where to look for price guides, yardage formulas, and your selling price point guidelines.

Each product topic is subdivided into sections in this chapter: hardline window coverings, soft-treatment window coverings, bedding and accessories, flooring, wallpaper, and upholstery. You will find measuring guidelines for each product and formulas and charts that will help you determine how much product it will take to do the job. You will also find relevant term glossaries and manufacturer source lists for each of the products. A section on putting together your sales manual will help you determine which of these materials to include. There are sample price lists and practice problems at the end of the chapter that will allow you to practice pricing each of the products before you actually go on an appointment.

Take the time to work the problems because doing so will help you feel more confident.

Section One: Hard-Line Window Coverings

This section covers all hard-line window coverings: blinds, shades, and shutters. The term hard-line refers to window coverings that are hard or durable in nature, unlike soft window treatments such as draperies and valances. We will start this section with a glossary so that when we discuss the specifics we will be using the same language.

Hard-Lines Glossary

CELLULAR SHADE. These are pleated shades where the fabric is double-layered and shaped like a honeycomb. Energy efficient, these come in many fabric choices, colors, and they range from transparent to opaque. Cellular shades are usually white on the side facing the street. They will fit into any window application: inside or outside mounts, arches, circles, skylights, and so on.

MINI BLIND. A blind that has metal slats running horizontally. Available in ½-inch, 1-inch, or 2-inch slats. Will work in most window situations, although they can become costly in odd-shaped windows. Slats can be adjusted for light control or the blind can be pulled up and down. Mini blinds are some of the least expensive window coverings on the market and are more commonly sold by big box stores than through custom businesses.

PLEATED SHADE. Shade consists of a single layer of fabric that is uniformly pleated. Shade can be pulled up and down only; there are no slats to adjust like a mini blind. Cost is usually between a mini blind and a cellular shade. Will fit most odd-shaped windows. Available in many colors, and fabrics range from transparent to opaque (although the opaque will still have light holes).

SHUTTERS. Available in 2-, 2½-, 3½-, and 4½-inch slats. Usually made from solid wood and painted or stained. Operates as a panel with adjustable slats. Can be customized to fit any window or style, depending on the size slat and the number of desired panels. Custom-built shutters can be very expensive, but are excellent at controlling light and heating and cooling. Most manufacturers will work with a customer's custom color.

WOOD BLIND. Available in 1-, 2-, and 3-inch slats and can be painted or stained to match existing woodwork. Approximately half the cost of shutters.

VERTICAL BLIND. A vertical running vane that is attached to a headrail. The vanes are constructed of aluminum, PVC, or fabric. The fabric vanes come freehanging or are inserted into a PVC backing. Available in 2-inch or 3½-inch vanes. Vanes can rotate 180 degrees or be pulled across track to open or close. Most commonly used in commercial settings, though there are new products on the market that have the functionality of a vertical (especially on a sliding door) but have the look of more attractive cellular shades. Price range is wide from very budget oriented to expensive, pattern and style dependent.

WOVEN WOODS. Shades made from natural fibers such as bamboo, rattan, or jute, which roll up or hang in roman shade style. Woven woods can be lined or unlined and embellished with color coordinated tapes to match the interiors. Price range is wide depending on the quality of the wood or grass and the embellishments.

Measuring for Hard-Line Products

Hardline treatments are installed either as inside or outside mounts, meaning it will either fit inside the window frame or be installed on the wall above the window or frame itself. With an inside mount the manufacturer will take the necessary deductions to ensure a proper fit, while an outside mount will be manufactured to your exact specifications.

You will have to pay attention to the window structure, the depth of the window, and what is around it. Inside mounted treatments cannot impede the function of the window and the window cannot impede the function of the treatment. If the window sash is flush with the frame, any blind or shade mounted inside the frame will not work properly. If the window has a shallow depth, the headrail on the shade may protrude out from the frame, which may not be the look you want. On the other hand, if the customer has stenciled around the outside of the window, you would want to fit the product on the inside so the stenciling wouldn't be covered up. Pay attention to the wall space around the window as well as the architecture itself. If the window has furniture or some other obstacle sitting right next to it, you won't be able to utilize that space for an outside mount.

With casement windows, the crank at the bottom of the window will be in the way if there is an inside mounted shade. As mentioned previously, sash windows need to have proper depth to successfully install an inside mounted shade.

On all the price lists you get from the manufacturers, there will be specifications of the products. It is imperative to know how each product is constructed because that information will come into play when you are considering the installation.

You should always use a good 1-inch steel tape measure (never a cloth tape). There will be times when you measure large windows, and anything less will not stand up. An inadequate tape measure will make measuring both awkward and inaccurate.

Always measure each window and don't assume that they are each the same size, even if the client or architect's plans says they are the same. Remember, you are measuring to the eighth of an inch and if you're over by an eighth of an inch on inside mounted treatments, they will not fit.

You have more leeway on outside mounts because they are installed directly onto the wall, but you still need to pay attention to the areas around the window. Make sure you have enough room for the brackets. There will be other obstacles, such as butting walls and low ceilings. It would be impossible to cover everything you will come up against because every house is built differently. Again, common sense will be your best-used tool when measuring. Finally, your manufacturers will likely offer education and materials around their products, which will include optimal applications, measuring tips, and more. Take full advantage of any information provided as each product is unique and one size definitely does not fit all.

This section includes measuring charts that will give you the general rules for measuring each product.

Measurement Instructions

Mini Blinds/Wood Blinds

(Inside Mount)

Width

Measure the width in three different locations (see fig. 1). Use shortest measurement.

Length

Measure the length in two to three different locations depending on width of window (see fig. 1). Use longest measurement.

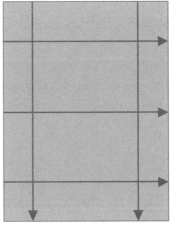

(Fig. 1)

Mini Blinds/Wood Blinds

(Outside Mount)

Width

Measure the exact width that you want covered. Add 3-4" if space allows for overlap to control light seepage (see fig. 2).

Length

Measure the exact length that you want covered. Add 4" (see fig. 2).

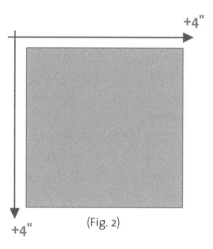

+4"

+4"

(Fig. 2)

Blinds on French Doors

Width

Measure the glass width plus a small overlap to cover the molding (watch for door knobs) (see fig. 3).

Length

Measure the glass length. Add 4" (see fig. 3).

Standard measurement for French Doors is 24" x 68".

When ordering, specify hold downs and spacers.

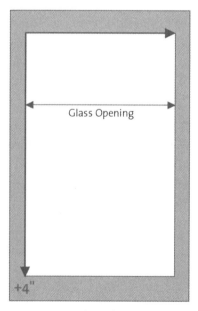

Glass Opening

+4"

(Fig. 3)

Vertical Blinds

(Inside Mount)

Width

Measure the width along top of window (see fig. 4).

Length

Measure the length in two places (see fig. 4). Use shortest measurement.

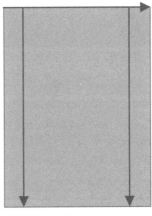

(Fig. 4)

Vertical Blinds

(Outside Mount)

Width

Measure the exact width that you want covered. Add 4" (see fig. 5).

Length

Measure the exact length that you want covered. Add 4" (see fig. 5).

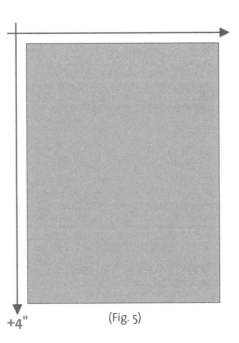

+4"   (Fig. 5)

Pleated Shades/Cellular Shades

(Inside Mount)

Width

Measure the width in three different locations (see fig. 6). Use shortest measurement.

Length

Measure the length in two different locations (see fig. 6). Use longest measurement.

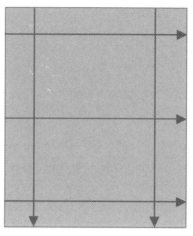

(Fig. 6)

Arch Window

(Perfect Arches)

Width

Measure the exact width (see fig. 7).

Length

Measure the exact center length. Length measurement should be exactly half the width for a perfect arch (see fig. 7).

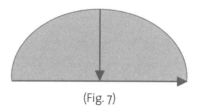

(Fig. 7)

When in doubt on arch windows, make a paper template.

Arch Window

(Nonperfect Arches)

Note: If the arch is a nonperfect arch, use an outside mount to avoid light gaps and bunching of material.

Width

Measure the exact width. Add 2" (see fig. 8).

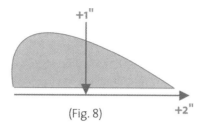

(Fig. 8)

Length

Measure the exact length. Add 1" (see fig. 8).

All Products

When you are covering just the square part of an irregularly shaped window, measure as you would for an inside mount.

When ordering: Order an inside mount with outside mount brackets.

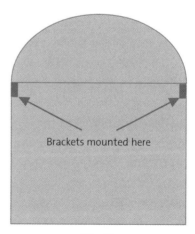

Brackets mounted here

(Fig. 9)

Sources

Please see appendix A for a list of window treatment resources that will get you started. You will be doing your own research as well to learn more about vendors and which you wish to be working with.

Section Two: Soft Treatments

The term *soft treatment* refers to draperies, valances, cornices, custom bedding, table rounds, and pillows. Basically, a soft treatment is any product that makes use of fabric. Your drapery workroom will fabricate all these products. This section offers tips and tricks for estimating yardage for soft furnishings but even the most experienced designers usually have their installer take the measurements and their workroom provide yardage estimates. The fabric and trim yardage must be exact as mistakes cost money! Order too little and you have to go back and order extra, or buy a whole new lot of fabric if you can't piece in an additional yard or two. And this will be on your dime; you can't go back to your client and ask for more money once you've quoted a price. Order too much and you've overcharged your client and your prices are artificially inflated. For estimating purposes on soft treatments, you will need to be able to figure labor and fabric costs, plus freight, tax, and installation. To start, you'll need to be familiar with the terms in the soft treatment glossary.

Soft Window Treatment Glossary

CASCADE. A piece of fabric that hangs in a zigzag line down the side or sides of a drapery treatment. It is sometimes double-sided with a contrast fabric.

CENTER DRAW. A pair of draperies that open and close from the middle.

CORNICE. A wooden boxlike structure covered with foam and then fabric. The edge can be straight, scalloped, or made to any shape you want.

CUSTOM-MADE DRAPERIES. Draperies made to individual specifications to fit a window.

CUT LENGTH. The length of the fabric after allowances have been made for the heading and the hem.

DRAPERY PANELS. Pinch pleat, tab top, rod pocket and grommet panels are all hung on a rod and can usually be opened or closed.

FINIALS. Decorative pieces on the end of a drapery rod such as balls or leaf-shaped designs.

FINISHED LENGTH. The actual length that the draperies will be when completed.

FULLNESS. A measurement of the drapery or valance that takes into account any necessary gathering. If a drapery is 250 percent or 2.5x full, there are 2.5 inches of fabric for every 1 inch of rod. Most custom draperies are 2.5x full, with a few exceptions. Most sheers are 3x full to increase privacy. Heavier fabrics are sometimes made at 2x fullness because they are so bulky. Flat valances are 1x full because they are not gathered.

JABOT. A cascade-like treatment that is used in the middle of swag treatments. It is usually one-half the length of cascades.

LINING. The backing used for a drapery. Most custom drapes are lined. There are also blackout linings to keep all light from seeping through the fabric and interlinings, which is an additional fabric sewn between the main fabric and lining to add fullness and stability to thinner fabrics such as silks.

ONE-WAY DRAW. A drapery that opens and closes from only one side. Most often used on a sliding glass door.

OVERLAP. The part of the center-draw drapery that is closest to the middle. It is what makes the pair overlap to avoid light gaps. It's usually 3½ inches on each side.

PANEL. One half of a pair of draperies. Used for one-way draws.

PATTERN REPEAT. All fabrics that have patterns have pattern repeats. The distance (in inches) between the start of a pattern to where it begins again is the measurement of the repeat. The larger the repeat, the more fabric it takes to match patterns.

RETURN. The distance between the face of a drapery and the wall. The average return for a drapery treatment is 3½ inches. Add 2 inches more for every over-treatment you add. For instance, if you are measuring for sheers, draperies, and a valance, plan for a 3½-inch return for the sheers, a 5½-inch return for the draperies, and a 7½-inch return for the valance. This return allows room for the under-treatments to move without getting caught in one another.

ROD POCKET. A hollow sleeve in the drapery or valance where the rod is to slide through.

SHIRRED DRAPERY. A drapery or valance in which the fabric is gathered along the rod.

SWAG. A valance in which the fabric is draped over a rod or attached to a board. The effect is a graceful flow of fabric. Used in conjunction with cascades and jabots.

TIEBACKS. Decorative hardware or pieces of fabric used to hold the drapery in place.

TRAVERSE ROD. A metal drapery rod with a pulley mechanism for drawing curtains.

VALANCE. A horizontal fabric treatment to be used with or without draperies.

WIDTH. A width of fabric is exactly that: one width of fabric (the actual width in inches varies). It is also a term used by drapery workrooms to arrive at their charges. When calculating a drapery cost, you will break it down into widths and yards. Use the width figure to determine the workroom cost and the yardage figure to determine the fabric cost.

Measuring and Calculating Yardage for Soft Treatments

The majority of the soft treatments (except fabric shades such as Romans, which should be treated the same as hard-line treatments) will be mounted on the outside of the window. Measure the window height from the top of the frame to the floor, the ceiling height, the total width including frame and from the sill to the floor, and the distance from the side of the window frame to a wall. When you design a drapery it will be up to you to determine how much wider and taller you want the draperies to be. You should figure a minimum of six inches on each side to eliminate any light gap (four if it's really tight), and four to six inches above the window to accommodate the drapery hardware. Other than that, there are no rules. Some customers may want to cover a window along with the entire wall to give the illusion of a wall-to-wall window; others may want to start the drapery just below the ceiling to add height to a room. Some customers will be on a budget, and you will be able to cut costs by just covering the area needed (the window) and adding the minimum number of inches.

Measuring for a valance is just as easy. You should measure the width of the window with frame and add four to six inches. The length will depend on the type of valance you are creating and the size of the window. Most valances range from twelve to thirty-six inches. If you are covering a small window, the valance should be on the shorter side, but if you are working with a large window you will wish a longer treatment. Pay attention to balance and scale.

If you are in doubt about the way your design will look on the window, you should draw it to scale on graph paper, which will also help your client visualize your design. You can make it come to life by using colored pencils that coordinate with the fabric colors the client has selected. You might also take a good photograph of the window and sketch your treatment design on the photograph. Finally, there are software programs available to help you design and estimate your window treatments. (See appendix A for details.) It's always a good idea to show your client a drawing of your design. It's amazing how two people can be talking about the same drapery but visualizing two entirely different treatments and you will want to avoid surprising your client when the treatments are installed. On the next few pages there are formulas and charts to help you estimate drapery, valance, bedding, tablecloth, and pillows. These will help you quote the job to a client, but take your measurements to your workroom and have them check your yardage before actually placing the order (especially on the first few jobs). It's important to note that if you are at all unsure about doing on-the-spot quotes, especially for big or complicated jobs, it is okay to bring it back to the customer in a day or so. You can set up a followup meeting, or call with the figures. While you may be slightly more likely to get a deposit on the spot than if you let it wait a day, dealing with incorrect pricing is a bigger deal in the long run.

Pinch-Pleat or Shirred Draperies (measure in inches)

To determine the number of widths:

Finished Width + 8" for side hems + 2 x Return = A

A x 2.5 (or desired fullness) = B

B ÷ 54 = number of widths (round up to nearest even number)

To determine the number of yards needed:

Finished length + 20" (for headers and hems) x number of widths = C

C ÷ 36 = number of yards

NOTE: This equation is based on a solid fabric with no pattern repeats. For every 10" vertical repeat, you should add an additional yard of fabric.

In addition to the design decisions and fabric selections, your quote will include:

- Drapery hardware, which will include decorative rods for drapes or functional hardware for traverse and other applications. Your manufacturer catalogues and websites will have detailed photos, installation instructions, and pricing.

- Lining materials including standard sateen linings, interlinings or blackout linings, or decorative contrast linings. Many workrooms include the standard sateen lining as part of their price to you, but if they don't you will need to include the pricing in your quote. In general, you will need as many yards lining as you do the face fabric.

- Labor costs to make the treatments.

- Installation cost.

- Don't forget shipping! If you are ordering your fabric and hardware from third-party vendors (as opposed to your workroom) you will be paying for all shipping costs. These costs should be part of your quote as they will eat significantly into your profits.

Tieback Yardage

A drapery can be held back with decorative tieback holders (they can be ordered through your drapery hardware source) or fabric ties. You can use the same fabric as the drapery or use a contrast fabric to add interest. A tieback is usually eighteen inches per width of fabric. Your workroom will charge you a price per pair, and your installer will also have a tieback installation charge. Add these charges together with the fabric requirements to arrive at your cost.

Figuring Swag Yardage and Labor

Swags can be draped over a rod or mounted on a board. As always, your workroom will provide you with their pricing for the job. The charges are usually figured per linear foot. You should line all swags because it will make them drape more easily. Add the price of the fabric, the price of the lining, the workroom labor charge, and the installation charge to determine your price. Add your markup to arrive at the retail price. Avoid using a heavy or stiff fabric because the swags will not drape as they should. Here is a guideline for the number of swags needed, determined by the width of the window and the yardage required to make them.

1 width	18" long
1½ widths	27" long
2 widths	36" long
2½ widths	45" long
3 widths	54" long

Swag Guideline and Yardage Chart

Face Width	up to 40"	41–70"	71–100"	101–120"	121–140"
Number of swags	1	1–2	3	3–4	4–5
Yardage	2	5	9½	9½	11½

Figuring Cascade Yardage

A cascade is a piece of fabric that falls at both ends of a swag. It can be self-lined, or a contrast fabric can be used. If you are self-lining the cascade, double the yardage on the following chart. If you are using a contrast lining, order the same amount as the face yardage. Your workroom will charge you per pair of cascades.

Cascade Yardage Chart

Length	up to 36"	37–48"	49–50"	61–81"	85–96"
Face width	1½	1½	2	2½	3

Figuring Rod Pocket Valances

Rod pocket valances are shirred (gathered) onto a rod. You can shirr the fabric onto the rod by itself or you can use a rod pocket as a header for a free-falling valance. Here are the formulas you need to determine the amount of widths and yardage that you will require.

Again, you will need to add the cost of the fabric, lining, workroom labor, drapery hardware, and installation to determine your cost.

(Always take measurements in inches)

To determine the number of widths

Rod width ÷ width of fabric = number of widths (round up to next even number)

To determine the number of yards

Finished length + [2 x (heading size + pocket size)] + 20 = length of cuts

Number of widths x length of cuts ÷ 36 = number of yards needed

Note: Add one pattern repeat per cut length for print fabrics.

Up the Roll versus Railroaded Fabrics

Normally fabric is milled so that the pattern runs "up the roll" and there are regularly placed vertical repeats of the pattern from beginning to end. Think of a floral motif where the big flower shows up every eighteen inches down the fabric piece. On a railroaded fabric, the pattern is running across the roll from beginning to end resulting in no vertical repeats (though it may have a horizontal repeat). Think of a striped fabric where the stripes run the entire length of the fabric. When using a print fabric with an up-the-roll pattern on a cornice, cushion, or sofa that is wider than the fabric (usually fifty-four inches), you need to piece the fabric together to accommodate the width. To avoid this piecing, which increases yardage needed and requires seaming that may not be preferable, you can use a railroaded fabric to run side to side. This also works with solid fabrics and very small, very regular prints, such as a check as well. This saves considerable fabric, time piecing, and seaming.

Cornice Boards

A cornice board is a decorative piece of wood that is covered with foam and fabric. It is a perfect way to add the softness of fabric into a room that utilizes straight lines. A cornice board will look great in offices or contemporary homes where flowery draperies won't work. All cornices should be lined. Your workroom will charge a fee per linear foot. You won't need drapery hardware for cornice boards because the boards are mounted directly onto the wall. Add the cost of the fabric, lining, workroom charges, and installation to arrive at your cost.

Yardage Calculator for Cornice Boards (measure all in inches)

Solid-Color Flat Cornices (fabric is railroaded)

Cornice face width + [returns x 4] (for two returns with fabric on outside and inside of the returns] = total number of inches = A

A ÷ 36 = yardage needed (round up to nearest yard)

Example: Finished width: 60" + (4" returns x 4 = 16") = 76 = A

A ÷ 36 = 2.1. Yardage needed is 3 yards.

Solid-Color Shirred Cornices (fabric is railroaded)

Cornice face width + [returns x 4] (for two returns with fabric on outside and inside of the returns] = total number of inches x 2.5 = A

A ÷ 36 = yardage needed (round up to nearest yard)

Example: Face width: 60" + (5" returns x 4 = 20") x 2.5 = 200 = A

A ÷ 36 = 5.5. Yardage needed is 6 yards.

Print or Patterned Cornices with repeat (fabric cannot be railroaded and if cornice width is greater than the fabric width, seaming will be required.)

Cornice face width + [returns x 4] (for two returns with fabric on outside and inside of the returns] = total number of inches = A

A ÷ 54 (standard width of decorator fabrics) to get the # of widths = B (round up to nearest yard)

Measure length at longest point and divide by the vertical pattern repeat measurement = C (round up) to get # of cuts to match the patterns across the width of the cornice.

C (# of cuts) x pattern repeat = D (number of inches needed to accommodate pattern matching)

D x B ÷ 36 = yardage required

Example: Face width: 60" + (4" returns x 4 = 16") = 76" total = A

A ÷ 54 = 1.4 rounded up to 2 widths = B

Cornice length: 20" ÷ 13" repeat = 1.5 cuts, rounded to 2 = C

C (2 cuts) x 13" repeat = 26 = D

D (26 inches) x B (2 widths) = 52 ÷ 36 = 1.4, rounded to 2 yards

Note that you will have to determine the returns measurement based on the individual cornice design.

Upholstery

Upholstery work is a natural way to increase your sales volume. When you are designing the draperies and selecting wallpaper in a room, it stands to reason that the furniture will need a new look.

Work with your client to select a coordinating fabric and then you can use the chart provided here to determine the number of yards needed. Note: This chart, like most charts of its kind, is based on plain-weave fabric. If your client has chosen a fabric with a pattern, you will need to adjust your figures based on the width of the pattern repeat. Call your upholsterer with the pattern repeat for help in determining the exact amount of extra fabric needed to get perfect pattern matches.

After you have a signed contract and a deposit, order the fabric and schedule a time for your upholsterer to pick up the furniture. When the furniture is complete, you will need to schedule another appointment for the upholsterer to drop off the furniture. When billing, take a deposit of between 50 and 75 percent on placement of order and collect the balance prior to delivery.

In addition to using this information, you will have to do much research on your own. These charts and formulas are meant to be only a guide to ease the process of estimating your projects. The more you do it, the quicker and more accurate the process is. Remember, if you're not sure, always go over your figures with your workroom before submitting a final quote to a client. Soft furnishings are a fun and challenging aspect of the design business. You can make a room look dramatic with a unique, bold drapery on the window, or you can make a room look cozy and inviting with different choices of textures and styles.

Upholstery Chart

Furniture	Yardage Needed
Sofa under 72" long	14 yards
Sofa over 72" long	15 yards
Sofa over 84" long	16 yards
Lounge chair	7–8 yards
Wing chair	7–8 yards
Recliner	7–8 yards
Barrel chair	7 yards
Dining room chair (seat only)	1 yard
Dining room chair (seat and back)	2–3 yards
Small bench	3–4 yards
Medium bench	4 yards
Large bench or ottoman	4–6 yards
Twin headboard	3 yards
Full headboard	3½ yards
Queen headboard	4 yards
King headboard	5 yards
California (CA) king headboard	6 yards

Section Three: Bedding and Accessories

Measuring

Adding custom bedding, pillows, and table rounds to an order can be quite profitable. It will add a custom look to a bedroom that is impossible to achieve with off-the-rack products. Your local workroom will include the price of these products on its price list. The standard sizes of mattresses has been included in this section to help you with the bedding measurements.

The measurements reflect width times length times drop (top of bed to top of box spring or floor). Keep in mind that you should ask customers to make the bed exactly like they will when they use the new bedspread or comforter. A thick blanket could make a lot of difference on how the bedding will fall, so always be sure to measure. When measuring for a bedspread or comforter, you must take the following measurements:

Bedspread Yardage Requirements

Size	48" or 54" fabric
Twin	8 yards
Full	8 yards
Queen	12 yards
King	12 yards
CA King	12 yards

Standard Mattress Sizes

Twin	39 x 75 x 21
Full	54 x 75 x 21
Queen	60 x 80 x 21
King	72 x 84 x 21
CA king	78 x 80 x 21

Yardage for Bedspreads

The following is the amount of fabric you will need for a standard throw bed-spread. The yardage is based on solid fabrics. For print fabrics, add two pattern repeats. There are many different styles of bedding, and they all have different yardage requirements. Be sure to ask your workroom for guidelines.

A dust ruffle, shams, throw pillows, and table rounds are also an easy add-on to your sale. The price of all these products can be figured quickly and easily. Following are some simple calculations for figuring yardage for these products.

Gathered-Style Dust Ruffle Yardage

The yardage requirements listed here are based on solid fabric that is gathered at 2.5x fullness.

Yardage for Pillow Shams

Yardage needed for flanged and corded shams is two yards. If you want a ruffle, add one yard for each ruffle. These yardage requirements are for shams measuring up to thirty-six by twenty-one inches. Again, there are many variations of pillow shams, so you will need to ask your workroom for specific quotes.

Dust Ruffle

Yardage Requirements

Size	Yardage
Twin	7½ yards
Full	8 yards
Queen	10 yards
King	11 yards
CA king	11 yards

Yardage for Throw Pillows

Round or square knife-edged 14-inch pillows require $\frac{1}{2}$ yard each. Add $1\frac{1}{2}$ yards for each self-lined ruffle. Ask your workroom for labor and pillow insert prices.

Yardage for Table Covers

For a round tablecloth up to 90 inches in diameter, you will need $5\frac{1}{2}$ yards. For a rectangular tablecloth up to 60 by 102 inches, you will need 6 yards. Add 2 yards if there is a ruffle.

Please see appendix A for a list of selected manufacturers of drapery and upholstery fabric, bedding and related accessories.

Section Four: Flooring

Among the types of flooring you will have to offer are carpet, wood, tile, and vinyl. As stated earlier, most of your flooring jobs will come from clients whose homes you are already designing. Because flooring manufacturers give special pricing to large carpet stores that do a lot of business, it will be nearly impossible for you to be competitive with them.

In the instances when the client is looking for carpet and shopping around for the best price, you probably won't get the job. But if you are working with a client and putting together a complete design package, then your prices will be in line with their entire budget and they will be less likely to price shop on individual items.

You should know the basics of flooring but it's not necessary for you to be able to bid a job to the exact yard. In the earlier discussion about contractors in chapter 7, you learned to make sure your flooring installer would measure your jobs and give you the amount of product needed. You will have the basic formula to give a rough estimate, and if the customer wants to proceed, you should have your installer measure the house and give you the exact numbers needed. From there you can present your final quote and close the sale. We will start this section with a glossary of terms for flooring as we did in the previous sections.

Flooring Glossary

BERBER. A Berber is a style of carpet that is not cut on top. The yarn forms little continuous loops. Available in solid colors or speckled patterns. Feels harder underfoot than thick plush carpets but wears better. Good for informal settings.

BROADLOOM. Carpets woven on a wide loom, generally twelve to thirteen feet wide, used for wall-to-wall applications. Includes Berbers and cut loops. Can also be cut and bound into smaller area rugs.

CUT BERBER. A softer Berber. Instead of loops, the yarn is cut. Wears almost as well as a Berber while still giving the look of casualness.

CUT-LOOP. A style of carpet that is mixed, with both small loops and cut yarn. Also known as *sculptured carpet*. Available in a variety of colors.

FLATWEAVE. A woven carpet with interlocking warp and weft threads. Produces a thinner, but still very sturdy product.

FRIEZE. The yarn on this type of carpet is twisted very tight, giving the appearance of a two-toned surface. This carpet is good for high-traffic areas because it won't show wear and you will not be able to see most footprints.

GROUT. A substance that is installed between tile and stone pieces. Available in many colors. The same color as the tile will give a smooth appearance, and a contrast color will give the area interest.

LAMINATE FLOORING. A synthetic flooring product that simulates the look of wood or stone.

PAD. A cushion that is installed under carpet. It makes the carpet softer to walk on and keeps the carpet looking new longer. Some carpets, such as Berber, have specific requirements for the type of pad needed to get the warranties. Ask your manufacturers for their requirements.

PLUSH. A carpet with a cut pile that is very rich in appearance. It is also called a *velvet*. The appearance is deceiving in this carpet because the yarn is not as dense as a Saxony and will not wear as well.

SAXONY. Like plush, this carpet also has a cut pile, but it is shorter. The yarns are packed closer together, which gives it greater wearability.

TILE. Ceramic tile is a manufactured product and is available in hundreds of colors and textures. Natural stone tile is cut from slate, marble, granite, and other hard stones. Tile squares can be laid on the floor, walls, or countertops. Sizes range from small mosaics up to twenty-four inches.

WOOD FLOORING. Natural wood planks in varying widths and species. Can come unfinished or prefinished and refinished over time.

Measuring for an Estimate

Following is a formula for square yardage to use when you are giving an estimate for flooring. You will also need to include padding (the same yardage as your carpet), installation (also figured by the yard), and any freight fee that the manufacturer charges.

Estimating Material Needs for Carpet, Wood Floors, Vinyl, Laminates, and Tile

Flooring is sold in either square feet or square yards.

1. Measure the width and length of each room to be covered. (Include closets and room cutouts but measure them as separate rooms.)
2. If you measured them in inches, convert to feet.
3. Multiply the width by the length and add 10 percent as a safety net.
4. Round up to the next nearest number. This is your square foot estimate.
5. If the product is sold in square yards, divide your footage number by nine.

For stairs:

1. Measure the width of a stair tread (horizontal measurement). Round up to nearest foot.
2. Measure the height of the riser and the depth of the tread (vertical measurements). Add these together and round up to the nearest foot.
3. Multiply the stair width by the combined riser and tread heights to come up with the total per stair measurement.
4. Multiply by the number of stairs, taking into account any landings.
5. Divide by nine to get to the square yardage amount.

See appendix A for a list of flooring vendors at different price points and product offerings.

Section Five: Wallpaper

Wallpaper Chart

Size of Room	Ceiling Height (in feet)			
	8	9	10	11
8 × 10	10	12	12	14
10 × 10	12	12	14	16
10 × 12	12	14	16	16
10 × 14	14	14	16	16
12 × 12	14	14	16	18
12 × 14	14	16	18	20
12 × 16	16	18	20	20
12 × 18	16	18	20	22
12 × 20	18	20	22	24
14 × 14	16	18	20	22
14 × 16	16	18	20	22
14 × 18	18	20	22	24
14 × 20	18	20	24	26
14 × 22	20	22	24	26
16 × 16	18	20	22	24
16 × 18	18	20	24	26
16 × 20	20	22	24	26
16 × 22	20	24	26	28
16 × 24	22	24	28	30
18 × 18	20	22	24	26
18 × 20	20	24	26	28
18 × 22	22	24	28	30
18 × 24	22	26	28	32

Wallpaper was out of fashion for quite a long time, but has roared back with a vengeance with modern designs and color palettes. Selling clients on the concept may not be difficult, but because there are so many patterns and styles to choose from it can be difficult to get them to make a final selection. Your job as a designer is to narrow down the vast array of choices to what works best for the space and design scheme and will be appealing to your client. Try to take as few books to the appointment as you can so as not to be overwhelming.

After your client has made the selection, measure the room to determine how many rolls you will need. Have your wallpaper contractor measure the room before you order it, just as you would for flooring. Some of the patterns are hard to match, and certain architectural aspects of a room may make a difference in the amount you need. The chart in this section gives general estimates.

Most of the wallpaper companies will require that you order the wallpaper in double or triple rolls: that is, two or three rolls at once. Some manufacturers will allow you to return unused rolls for a restocking fee so check with your manufacturer to determine their policy. Make sure that you know whether the wallpaper is priced or sold in single, double, or triple rolls.

Due to the prevalence of online discounters, most wallpaper companies use different product codes for papers sold in retail stores than the actual wholesale product code. Since consumers like to get the best price, it's not uncommon for some to look through books in a store, write down product codes and search online for discounted product. The coding method tries to protect retail vendors from this practice.

See appendix A for a list of wallpaper resources at different price points and product offerings.

Section Six: Miscellaneous Products

You never know what you will run up against when planning the design of a home. Let's imagine that you are upholstering some kitchen chairs for a client who has five children. In that case, you may want to suggest that you laminate the fabric to protect it against spills and stains. Or you may have a client who wants you to coordinate artwork with the new design of a room. Where do you look for such items? Please refer to appendix A for a list of miscellaneous resources that you may find helpful.

The Internet Is Your Go-To Resource.

The companies you will be continuously using in your business have websites that are crammed with current information for your benefit. Use these sites regularly to stay up to date on trends, colors, styles, and so on. Research regularly and you will find new, innovative products and designs that may appeal to a particular client.

Sustainability in Interior Design

This is a good place to mention that you, as an interior designer, should be ready and eager to implement environmentally sustainable decorating concepts. No matter what the design style preference, there is something that you can do to promote "green" design—reduce, reuse, recycle, and recover. Be sure to read articles, search the Internet, and shop your local bookstore to add to your library of information.

There are many ways to green your home or your client's home. Here are a few suggestions:

- **Roofing:** Traditional standing seam metal, metal shingles, cedar shake shingles, slate, tile, concrete tiles, recycled rubber. All of these roof materials can be green; many are made from recycled materials. Check your suppliers and ask questions.

- **Siding:** Hardi-plank, fiber cement siding, metal siding, either aluminum or steel siding (many are made from recycled products), engineered wood siding.

- **Windows:** Double-paned windows with low-e coating on glass reflect heat back into the home during winter months. Check with your local window distributors and get information on what is offered to best serve your area of the country. Again, use the Internet for more research.

- **Heating and cooling systems:** Energy saving and properly sized HVAC units, tankless water heaters, and solar panels. Geothermal is another possibility. Geothermal heat pumps (geoexchange or ground-source heating and cooling) can be the most expensive system initially for a home. Upon completion it can become the biggest in benefits of energy savings and environmental consciousness. This system uses the earth's natural below-surface temperature to heat and cool the home. With a constant ground temperature of approximately 55 degrees year-round, less energy is needed to cool for summer or heat for winter use. Contact a qualified installer. Do your research!

- **Eco-friendly insulation:** There are some exciting new products on the market. Recycled cotton denim (your old jeans!), sheep-wool insulation (not easily available in the United States), Icynene spray-in foam, Aerogel (a special superporous silicon foam that is 99 percent air), Air Krete (a nontoxic, environmentally friendly, fireproof, and sound absorbing material that is also low in volatile compounds [VOCs]), cellulose, spray polyurethane foam, and eco-friendly fiberglass.

- **Rainwater collecting:** Rainwater used for yard purposes only can be captured from your roof. This water is channeled through gutters and downspouts into a storage tank located either above ground or below ground. The home owner will need a method to distribute the water as needed. Also, choose plants for the yard that thrive in your soil and climate conditions. These plantings require much less water to survive.

- **Lighting:** Replace regular light bulbs with compact fluorescent bulbs, and change outdoor security lighting to high-efficiency bulbs. Use either a higher efficiency incandescent or watt misers, compact fluorescent or mercury vapor bulbs. Use sensors for outdoor lighting, install dimmer switches when needed, and use cordless area lights. Check on LED lighting with your lighting supply store for placement in the home. One great area to use LED lights is for your holiday lighting. And it will save you a ton of money.

- **Paints:** Many paint companies have paint low in VOCs. Go to www.green seal.org and you will find a list of companies that have paints that are environmentally safe.

- **Flooring:** This category covers carpet, wood, tile, and a host of materials. You can find reclaimed wood, natural cork, and bamboo flooring. There are many natural stone tiles available. Carpet manufacturers have natural fibers such as organically grown cotton and wool. Some fibers are made from recycled materials. Use the Internet to do more research, and ask your carpet representative about the green products his or her company offers. You can learn a lot from the reps.

- **Wallpapers:** Eco-friendly wallpaper is also available. These papers are printed on formaldehyde-free paper using water-based inks. They do not contain lead or other heavy metals and have very low VOC levels. The papers should be installed with a traditional wheat paste or cellulose paste, which are VOC-free. All you have to do is get on the Internet and type in "eco-friendly wallpapers." This will bring up many company sources for you to choose the one that meets your requirements.

There is no end to what can be green in the home. This is just the beginning. Each client will have different needs and requirements. Use your creativity to help them reclaim, reuse, and enjoy some of their existing possessions. Many of these green improvements will be new sales for you, even if it is just finding an old piece that fits their requirements.

To find eco-friendly furniture, check out www.sustainablefurnishingscouncil. org. On this site you can get a list of companies with furniture that meet environmentally safe requirements. The list is extensive and growing steadily. Check it often, and you will find a variety of items to meet any need you may have.

Technology is continually evolving and new products are becoming available regularly. If you are involved in a new construction, take it from the roof to the ground outside and then turn to the interior for more ways to green the structure. Most of us will be part of a remodel. In this instance, use the same approach: Research the Internet and then find a local contractor or supplier to accomplish your goal. Remember: reduce, reuse, recycle, and recover. Have fun with this approach, and you will surprise yourself with many new ideas.

Sales Manual

An organized sales manual will make your appointments run smoother, because you will know exactly where to find the formula or price chart that you are looking for. You can go old-school with a simple three-ring binder organized to suit your needs, or create your files in digital format to bring up quickly on a tablet or laptop computer. You could even create your own calculators in a spreadsheet to aid in your on-the-spot estimating. Your manufacturer's price charts and information should be included. These may already be available in digital format or you could scan in the paper copy for your digital files.

Copy or scan the charts and formulas from this book as well as any others you have collected and add them accordingly to your sales manual.

Once you have negotiated the discounts with your manufacturer and arrived at your retail selling price for each of the products, prepare a separate list for each section with your retail selling prices. There will be clients who will ask you to negotiate your prices, so include your high and low range so you will be prepared to negotiate.

Include any measuring instructions you may need and have blank forms available to guide you in your measuring process. There are many different ways of doing the same job, you just have to find what works best for you and turn it into your own formula. Try not to reinvent the wheel each time you do a project—your forms and charts will help you save time and reduce the potential for error.

Finally, add any photos or illustrations that will help you express your ideas to clients more easily. Again, these can be kept in a digital photo album which can be easier to carry around and refer to.

You Are on Your Way

This chapter isn't meant to be your only training in the design business; it only covers the very basic rules of the main products you will be working with. You can and should ask your manufacturer's representative for more detailed training and information—their job is to help you sell their product and you can learn a great deal from them. Take a course. Read more books. Do everything that you can to ensure your confidence and success before you walk into your first appointment. Be sure you know what you're doing before you take on a design project. But never be afraid to say that you don't know something and you will need to do some research and get back to a client or a rep. The old saying "measure twice, cut once" needs to be your constant mantra. Interior designers and sales people need to know a great deal of information about a great many different products, plus how to incorporate them into a beautiful and functional interior that pleases the client. It's always better to be honest and take a moment to check on a detail than have to back track or eat the cost later on.

Practice Worksheets

On the following pages there are sample price lists and practice problems. Use these to get familiar with the bidding process for each of the products. The answer key is located in Appendix B at the back of the book.

Practice Problems

Discounts

Your manufacturer discounts for the purposes of these exercises are as follows:

1. Mini Blinds   52 percent discount (cost factor)
2. Cellular Shades   55 percent discount (cost factor)
3. Vertical Blinds   49 percent discount (cost factor)
4. Drapery and Upholstery Fabrics   Less 50
5. Wallpaper   50

Carpet, tile, and vinyl are priced at wholesale prices.

Questions

1. A customer has windows that measure as follows:

    (three) $26\frac{1}{8}" \times 69\frac{7}{8}"$
    (seven) $45" \times 90"$
    (one) $11\frac{1}{2}" \times 72"$

The customer wants to put mini blinds in the windows. What is your cost?

2. Figure the price for a cellular shade that measures 43 by 68 inches. What would the price difference be if the shade came as two on one headrail?

3. Figure the price of an arch cellular shade that measures 30 by 15 inches.

4. Figure the price of a mini blind that measures 32 by 64 inches. What would the price difference be if the customer wanted the controls on the left side instead of the standard right side?

Mini Blind Retail Price Chart

Length up to:	Width to: 23"	26"	29"	32"	36"	41"	45"	48"	54"
54"	$125	135	146	155	164	173	184	195	215
61"	$136	147	158	169	178	189	199	211	223
68"	$144	155	164	173	182	193	210	224	236
71"	$150	161	170	181	193	209	222	231	241
78"	$161	172	183	191	207	220	231	242	253
84"	$173	182	193	205	226	237	248	257	268
91"	$189	198	213	221	233	244	256	267	278
97"	$199	211	225	234	244	255	267	278	289
103"	$210	221	233	242	251	263	275	286	297

Note: For two or three blinds on one headrail, add a $145 surcharge. For blinds under 12", add a $40 surcharge. No charge for alternate control locations.

Cellular Shade Retail Price Chart

Length up to:	Width to: 24"	30"	36"	43"
36"	$78	96	114	121
41"	$90	107	125	133
48"	$100	116	130	142
54"	$112	127	141	154
61"	$123	138	154	166
68"	$136	149	167	178

Note: For bottom-up/top-down shade, add a 50 percent surcharge. For arch-top shade, add a $55 surcharge. For skylight shade, add a $130 surcharge. For two or three shades on one headrail, add a $50 surcharge.

Vertical Blind Retail Price Chart

Length up to:	Width to: 26"	38"	52"	64"	76"	84"	89"	100"
60"	$210	290	366	450	515	577	599	632
Insert	180	236	296	334	389	431	451	487
73"	240	326	414	489	571	632	659	741
Insert	191	251	318	361	420	458	470	538
84"	260	356	452	535	627	702	723	810
Insert	220	370	331	374	439	489	510	571

Drapery and Upholstery Fabric Retail Price Chart

Pattern	Price per yard	Uses	Content	Width
Spring	$26.90	Drapery	50/50 Poly/Cotton	48"
Summer	$27.10	Drapery	100% Cotton	54"
Autumn	$37.20	Upholstery	100% Cotton	54"
Winter	$47.45	Upholstery	100% Cotton	54"

Wallpaper Retail Price Chart

Pattern	Price per Single Roll
Plaid	$15.75
Stripe	$16.25
Floral	$17.10
Check	$19.00
Border	$11.99

Note: Wallpaper must be ordered in double rolls. Borders may be ordered in single rolls.

Carpet and Vinyl Wholesale Price List

Name	Price per Square Yard	Style
Contempo	$8.99	Carpet
Adobe	$9.50	Carpet
Country	$11.99	Vinyl
Eclectic	$13.98	Vinyl

Tile Wholesale Price List

Style	Price per Square Foot
Gloss	$1.20
Matte	$1.57
Stone	$1.99
Textured	$2.98

Note: Tile must be purchased in boxes of 45 square feet each.

5. A customer has a window with a fabulous view. She wants a cellular shade that operates from the bottom up so she can enjoy privacy without losing the view. The window measures 36 by 60 inches. How much is your cost?

6. A customer wants to put a mini blind on an extremely large window. The window panes are broken up into three sections. The window measures 54 by 103 inches. What is the best application for this window?

7. A customer has a sliding glass door that he wants to put vertical blinds on. The measurement is 75 by 84 inches. The customer has a severe sun problem. What is the best application and how much is your cost?

8. You are figuring your cost for upholstering a customer's sofa. The sofa measures 78 inches long. Use the fabric Winter. You know that your labor cost is $250. What is your total cost? (*Hint:* Use the upholstery chart on page 150.)

9. What is your cost on a 6-foot cornice board with 3-inch returns made out of the fabric Summer? (It is a solid.) Your labor cost is $10 per linear foot. Your installation charge is $3 per linear foot, and your lining cost is $4 per yard.

10. What is your cost for a swag and cascade treatment made out of the fabric Winter on a window that measures 75 inches? How many swags should you use? Your cascades measure 36 inches in length and are con-

trast-lined with the fabric Summer. Your workroom labor is $20 per linear foot, your installation charge is $3 per linear foot, and your lining cost is $4 per yard.

11. What is your cost for a pinch-pleat drapery that measures 40 by 84 inches? Use the fabric Autumn with a lining that costs $4 per yard. Your workroom charges $75 per width. Your installer charges $5 per linear foot. Your drapery hardware will cost $54.70.

12. You are designing an entire bedroom. Figure the price for a king-size throw bedspread that uses the fabric Summer. The workroom labor is $180. Also figure the price of the fabric for two corded pillow shams that measure 34 by 18 inches out of the fabric Spring. Figure out how much the fabric would cost to add three 12-inch round pillows with a ruffle in the fabric Autumn.

13. You have measured a house for carpet and tile. The measurement for the room in which the carpet is to be installed is 12 by 15 feet. The measurement for the room in which the tile is to be installed is 10 by 12 feet. The customer has selected Adobe for the carpet and Stone for the tile. Your cost for the pad is $2 per yard. Your installer charges $4 per yard for the carpet and $40 per hour for the tile (the job will take about three hours). What is your total cost?

14. What is your cost to wallpaper a room that measures 18 by 20 feet with 8-foot ceilings using the pattern Stripe? The customer also wants to add a border all the way around the room. How many rolls should you order?

NOTE: All prices referenced in these practice questions are for the purposes of practice only and do not represent real-world pricing.

10 Managing the Growth of Your Business

There comes a time in every business when the owner starts to realize that he or she needs help. This is the time when you will need to step back and analyze your business situation. Think of this stage as a fork in the road; the route you decide to take will forever impact your life and business. Sound scary? It can be if you're not prepared for it. You should have some idea when you start your business about how large you want it to become. At some point you will have to decide whether you want to stay a small, one-person operation or continue to grow into a larger, more profitable business, taking into account the effect on your home life.

It is possible in this type of business to have a few employees while still working out of your home. You are not likely, however (although anything is possible), to cultivate a large number of builder or commercial accounts while operating out of your home as you may be seen as too small to handle larger scale projects. Plus, there are liability issues involved that are better handled in a commercial space. If that is your goal, part of your long-term plan should include a move into a retail or office space. If your main goal is residential design work, you have more flexibility. As most of your contact with customers will be in their home, keeping a home office is a practical way to keep costs down. But if you wish to hire several employees or take on an intern, you will eventually want to strongly consider a commercial space.

Moving Out

Operating a home-based business has more advantages than one can count, such as no commute to and from an office, wearing your casual comfies when not meeting with clients, a feeling of independence, and so on. But there comes a time in most businesses when the owner has to decide whether or not to move the business to an office or retail location. Read through this small checklist. If at any time in the course of your business you can answer yes to even one of these questions, you may want to consider moving out.

Here are some tips for managing the growth of your business when you just can't do it all alone.

1. When you get to the point where you know you are losing money because you can't handle all the tasks required to run your business on your own, it may be time to take on some help. Hiring a bookkeeper to handle your financial paperwork is often the first item designers will delegate, but you may find you'd rather source out schematic drawings or managing your sample programs. The point is, delegate the tasks you least like to do and keep your favorite jobs for yourself.

2. Once you have enough business, you can start converting contract laborers into full-time employees. You will have to do your individual numbers, but you should save money and time by paying the contractors a set fee or salary.

3. If your design consulting business is truly booming, you may want to bring on an assistant designer. Unlike an administrative assistant, an assistant (or associate) designer will handle his or her own design projects and meet with clients. You can hire an experienced designer who requires no training, or you can hire an inexperienced person whom you will train to do things your way (more about this later).

4. If you have four or more sales associates working for you, you may need to hire a sales manager (or promote one of your sales people and hire a new one). The sales manager can sell a limited number of jobs while taking care of the everyday business tasks and keeping your sales team on task.

Checklist: Do You Stay or Do You Go?

	Yes	No
You have too many employees to work comfortably.	___	___
You're running into zoning problems (i.e., too many cars come and go).	___	___
You are interested in builder and commercial accounts, but they want you to have an office.	___	___
You've simply outgrown your space.	___	___
Your work is interfering with your family life.	___	___

Finding Good Employees

Perhaps one of the most challenging aspects of growing your business is finding good, qualified people to fill new positions. As a business owner, your goal will be to get the best results for the smallest amount of advertising dollars spent. The way that you advertise for prospective employees will largely depend on where you live. If you live in a small town to midsize city you likely have a local newspaper that is widely read. Classified rates are usually not too expensive and you will also get the benefit of having your ad posted to their online pages as well. If you live in a large city, classified rates can be astronomical and not an efficient way to get to the right people in any event. These days, most job ads are placed online on places like Craigslist.com, your local paper's online classifieds, Monster.com, Careerbuilder.com, or possibly LinkedIn. You might also try a local design school if hiring a design assistant as well. Most professional trade organizations have student chapters and offer a spot for job postings on their websites as well. Be sure to list your job openings on your website, blog, or other social media sites as well. Because interior design is a glamour profession, it's not difficult to attract applicants for any job you are offering. The trick is to attract the right applicants.

If you are advertising for a bookkeeper or an office assistant, the ad should be very straightforward and to the point. For an office assistant, it might read something like this:

> *Part-time help needed for small business. Duties will include*
> *answering phone, filing, ordering materials, and scheduling.*
> *Will train. Possibility for advancement in the future. Email your*
> *resume and cover letter to: me@myweburl.com*

You may or may not wish to say that you're a design business in your ad for straight administrative work. While your entire staff should be interested in the business you're in, you don't necessarily want to have a designer wanna-be who is more interested in doing design work than administrative tasks.

When you advertise for designers, the ad can be a little more creative. You will want to outline the importance of professionalism while highlighting the creative aspects of the job. You might use the following ad if you are advertising for an inexperienced designer:

> *Small design firm now hiring associate designer to assist*
> *with residential design projects. Position requires professional*
> *demeanor, knowledge of CAD [computer-aided design]*

applications, interest in working with luxury goods, attention to detail and sales ability. Email your resume and cover letter to: me@myweburl.com

The Interview Process

Think back to the times when you've been interviewed by a potential employer. You were probably nervous, and it was generally the circumstances of the interview that made the difference in whether or not you felt it was successful. If an employer was interviewing for an accounting position, the interview would be a lot more straightforward than if the interview were for a designer position. As the employer, it will be up to you to set the stage.

Before you conduct your first interview, you should make a list of the traits you are looking for. For instance, if you are interviewing for a designer position, the following traits may apply: outgoing personality, good with people, trustworthy, good with details, fast thinker, professional dresser, responsible, confident.

Form your interview questions around the traits that you desire. If you are looking for an experienced designer, you will need to throw in specific questions about product and technique and you will wish to see their portfolio of work. If you have narrowed the selection down to a few good people, you might want to give them a test, such as the one in the products chapter, to determine how much they really know or can learn quickly. Once you have narrowed your selection down to two applicants, you will want to check their professional references. Never skip this step and always ask as a final question, "Would you hire this candidate again if given the opportunity?" If the reference dances around the question and doesn't really answer, that may be telling you something. These days, people and businesses are afraid to give a bad reference for fear of being sued, so it's important to pay attention to other things such as how quickly they returned your call or email—which can indicate how much they want to help the applicant. If they are unwilling to say anything more than confirm dates of employment, this may be a negative sign.

Probationary Period

It's a good idea to hire someone with the understanding that it's on a probation basis. If you are hiring an experienced applicant, a three-month probation period should be enough time to establish whether or not he or she will work out. If you are training someone, six months is a reasonable amount of time. Remember, it costs money every time you hire and train an employee, so you will want to give the new person every chance possible to succeed at the job.

Noncompete Agreements

Aspiring new designers will sometimes apply for jobs, then work just long enough to get on-the-job training, business contacts, and a supply of samples. Then they leave to start businesses of their own. This works out well for the new designers, but not for the employer!

The best way to avoid this is to use noncompete agreements. The agreement should be drawn up by an attorney and signed on the first day of employment. The agreement protects you against a designer who would use you for training, become friendly with your customers, and then leave to start his or her own business, taking some of your clients along. By signing the agreement, designers promise not to go into a competing business (for themselves or for one of your competitors) for a predetermined amount of time. It also sets guidelines for after the time is up. It will restrict how geographically close to your business they can open theirs. Different states have different rules about these types of agreements, so it's vital to consult an employment attorney on the matter and have the attorney draw up the contract. Ultimately, though, you need to accept that your assistant may well go out on his or her own when the time is right, and it's a perfectly normal thing. You should be supportive of this and not try to hold your assistant back, without letting him or her walk off with your best clients.

What to Pay

If you are hiring a bookkeeper, office help, or contractor, you will have to pay the going rates in your area. It's simple enough to determine the rates—just look in the paper to see what other companies are offering. Try to hire the best possible candidate for what you can afford. When it's time to hire designers, you have a few more options. You can pay a designer one of three ways: salary, commission, or salary plus commission.

Salary

If your new design assistant is working directly under you and has little to no one-on-one relationship with your clients outside of tasks you assign them, then a straight salary is the way to go. Since commissions are used as the "carrot" to motivate employees to bring in more revenue, it doesn't make sense to offer a commission to an employee who isn't in a revenue-generating position.

Commission Only

For a small business, this is the most affordable way to bring in extra sales help without being tied to a salary. You should pay the designer 10 to 15 percent of his or her gross sales. Let's say that you offered the designer a straight 10 percent commission. The designer would have to sell $15,000 per month to make $1,500 per month in commission, which totals $18,000 per year. To afford this, you should have enough business to support yourself, your business, and the new employee. Most commission-only jobs are work for hire versus a true employee situation. If you want this person to be hired as part of your staff and available to you whether or not you have business, then you will likely have to offer them a draw on commission, which is a preset small hourly rate that is deducted from future sales.

Salary Plus Commission

Let's imagine that you still plan to offer the new designer 10 percent of her or his gross sales as an incentive. You might offer a $1,500 guaranteed salary plus 10 percent commission on any amount over $15,000 in sales. You would be paying the same amount as in the commission-only example except that the first $1,500 would be guaranteed regardless of whether the designer sold $15,000. If you don't have at least $15,000 per month in excess business, you're not ready to hire a designer. Remember, employee expenses go well beyond salaries. They also include employer taxes, worker's compensation insurance, healthcare, and other benefits.

Quotas

To keep specific goals in mind, you should set up quotas for your sales staff. As they begin to reach and exceed their quotas, you should reevaluate and reset the quota levels as needed to continue to grow. You might offer small rewards along the way as quotas are exceeded such as a gift certificate to a nice restaurant or sports tickets.

Yet another way to motivate your employees is to offer them a bonus for harder-to-reach goals. For instance, if your employees' quota is $15,000 per month, you can set an optional advanced quota of $22,000. If they reach this higher goal, they will be rewarded with a 15 percent commission on everything over and above the first $15,000. (This would mean that instead of making $2,200 that month, their salary would be $2,550.) The harder goal motivated them to sell more, and you earned a profit on the $7,000 in increased sales.

Gas Allowance

Some design firms offer to pay for their designers' gas. Because of the nature of the business, it's not unusual for a designer to use two tanks of gas per week. If you want to reimburse your employees, simply ask for a mileage log and receipts for gas used at work. This little step will go a long way in employee satisfaction.

Keeping Designers Motivated

As in every job, it's easy to get frustrated and feel unappreciated. A little encouragement goes a long way in keeping most employees motivated. If one of your designers overcame many obstacles and finally signed a large job, you'd want to acknowledge the achievement—anything from an office lunch at the down-the-street eatery to a congratulations party, complete with champagne.

Another easy way to motivate your employees is to include them in the manufacturers' spiffs (promotional contests). They will give you a small sum for every product sold from a particular line. It can be beneficial for you to pass this incentive along to your employees as a motivational tool that will also enhance your bottom line.

Hiring a Sales Manager

As your business grows, especially if you're a product-focused business, you may need a sales manager to supervise your staff and relieve yourself of that part of the operation. He or she can handle the day-to-day work and take over any responsibilities that a part-time office assistant would do, such as ordering materials and scheduling appointments and installations. The sales manager can even sell a few jobs when there's time. You can pay the manager a small salary, with an override on the total gross sales. Thus, part of the manager's responsibility will be to increase your sales. He or she will do so by keeping the designers motivated and by personally marketing builders and large accounts. You must be ambitious and willing to work a lot of hours to accomplish this level of business, but it can be done.

Training Your Employees

Training your employees is vital to their success as well as the success of your business. The more training your employees have, the better they will perform their jobs. Training instills confidence, and confidence translates into increased sales.

Ask your manufacturers' representatives to give your employees in-depth training on their products. If you ask each representative to do this, your employees will be well on the way to a great understanding of all the products. Send your employees to seminars that are held by the various manufacturers and trade associations. Most manufacturers will hold free seminars that introduce new products (or simply go over the old ones) at least once a year. Most trade associations offer classes and give the designers certification awards for completing them. There is usually a fee for these classes, but they are well worth the expense. Encourage your designers to take classes in design. You may even want to consider reimbursing them for half or even all of the tuition costs. Remember, the better trained and supported they are, the more they will sell—and fewer costly mistakes will be made. You might also encourage your staff to join networking groups to enhance your marketing efforts and it's worth paying for their membership dues or event tickets. You just have to be sure that they are always there to represent your business, not themselves personally.

You Can Do It!

Now that you've learned the basics, it's time to put your new knowledge into practice. The interior design business is one of the few that can be started on a limited budget while still having enormous growth potential. Now that you know what many designers learned the hard way, your odds of success are greatly enhanced. May your new life as a home-based interior designer be full of fun as well as prosperity. Good luck!

Appendix A: Resources

Associations and Resources

Listed below are the major organizations, associations and resources you will want to get to know.

General Design & Builder Associations

American Society of Interior Designers (ASID)

asid.org

ASID is the leading organization for interior design professionals.

International Furnishings and Design Association (IFDA)

ifda.com

610-992-0011

IFDA brings together professionals in the furnishing and design industries. It seeks to enhance networking between the two industries as well as cross-industry education and professional development.

International Interior Design Association (IIDA)

iida.org

888-799-4432

IIDA is a global community of interior design professionals and innovators. The association provides a forum to showcase the impact of design on health, safety, and well-being while balancing good design with best business practices.

National Association of Home Builders (NAHB)

nahb.org

800-368-5242

Since 1942 this trade association has been promoting policies that make housing affordability, availability, and choice a national priority.

United States Green Building Council (USGBC)

Leadership in Energy and Environmental Design (LEED)

800-759-1747

usgbc.org/leed

Education and information about sustainability in architecture and design.

The Codes Guidebook for Interiors, 6th Edition

Sharon K. Harmon, Katherine E. Kennon.

Wiley Publishing, 2007

Window Coverings Associations & Resources

DraperyPro

DraperyPro.com

An online professional networking forum that concentrates on the issues of soft window coverings.

Window Covering Association of America (WCAA)

wcaa.org

240-404-6490

A nonprofit trade association of dealers, decorators and workrooms dedicated to the retail window coverings industry.

Wallcoverings Association (WA)

wallcoverings.org

312-321-5166

A nonprofit trade association representing wall coverings manufacturers, distributors, and suppliers to the industry. The association provides a communication channel between segments of the industry while also promoting the use of wall coverings.

Workroom Association of America (WAOA)

waoamembersite.com

254-662-4021

The WAOA was formed to support artisans in the soft coverings industry by providing benefits, value added programs, and a voice to its members.

Custom Home Furnishings Academy

chfindustry.com

CHFA began as a school for drapery education. Today they offer a variety of educational opportunities focused on all aspects of window treatment, upholstery, and interior design, as well as professional workrooms.

E-Z Decorator

ezdecorator.com

E-Z Decorator offers an interior design visualization tool that allows users to create floor plan layouts without computer software or hand drawing designs by providing a huge selection of premade drawings and templates in a large variety of styles.

The Design Directory of Window Treatments

Jackie Von Tobel

Gibbs Smith, 2007

jackievontobel.com

The Design Directory of Bedding

Jackie Von Tobel

Gibbs Smith, 2009

jackievontobel.com

The Encyclopedia of Window & Bed Fashions

Randall International, 2014

CRI Corporate

PO Box 1656

Orange, CA 92856

714-771-8488

randallonline.com

Window Fashions Magazine

651-330-0574

wf-vision.com

Precision Draperies

draperyeducation.com

A custom drapery and soft treatment workroom located in Denver, Colorado. Their services allow you to tailor draperies to your needs. They also offer publications, software, and training.

Soft Design Lab
softdesignlab.com
From Jackie Von Tobel and Deb Barrett, education, inspiration, online learning. This creative community will help you master the art of designing soft furnishings.

Sustainable Furnishings Council
sustainablefurnishingscouncil.org
This educational and marketing organization promotes a healthy environment by assessing the environmental impact of the furniture produced by its member companies.

Textile Fabric Consultants
textilefabric.com
Supplier of fabric swatch kits used in teaching textiles.

Carpet, Tile and Flooring Associations and Resources
The Carpet & Rug Institute (CRI)
carpet-rug.org
706-278-3176
A good source for education and technical information on everything from health and environmental efforts to quality standards and durability.

Marble Institute of America (MIA)
marble_institute.com
440-250-9222
The leading source of information on standards for natural stone workmanship, practice, and products. The MIA disseminates educational information for architects and construction specification professionals and offers accreditation for installers and fabricators of natural stone products.

National Tile Contractors Association (NTCA)
tile-assn.com
601-939-2071
The NTCA is a nonprofit trade organization representing professionals throughout the tile and stone industries including manufacturers, distributors, contractors, architects, designers, and builders.

North American Laminate Floor Association (NALFA)

nalfa.com

202-785-9500

NALFA is a trade association dedicated to the laminate flooring industry. They provide a national directory of laminate flooring installers and inspectors as well as advice on laminate choices, standards, and performance.

Tile Council of North America (TCNA)

tcnatile.com

864-646-8453

TCNA promotes the use of ceramic tile by researching, developing, and testing installation materials and methods. The organization works with regulatory and trade agencies to develop and publish the various tile industry installation standards and guidelines.

World Floor Covering Association (WFCA)

wfca.org

800-624-6880

A source for information on all types of flooring; dedicated to helping consumers make informed flooring decisions. Website includes flooring estimate calculators.

Floorfacts

floorfacts.com

Floorfacts.com provides valuable information on all types of flooring to help consumers make educated decisions about their flooring options and find the right flooring manufacturers.

Color Associations and Resources

Color Association of the United States (CAUS)

colorassociation.com

212-947-7774

Produces an annual report that forecasts upcoming colors for most interior design products, fashion, and marketing. Offers e-learning opportunities, webinars, and workshops in color education.

The Color Marketing Group (CMG)

colormarketing.org

703-329-8500

The CMA is a nonprofit international association of color design professionals focused on the exchange of information on color trends and combinations between color professionals.

International Association of Color Consultants/Designers—North America (IACC-NA)

iaccna.com

740-272-1072

The English-language chapter of the ICAA, made up of color professionals from around the world. The ICAA is dedicated to the use of color and accredits architects, interior designers, environmental designers, color psychologists, marketing specialists, and other color professionals.

Pantone

https://pantone.com

866-PANTONE

Pantone is the world-renowned authority on color and provides technology for the selection and accurate communication of color across a variety of industries and media.

Trade Shows

Architectural Digest Home Design Show

archdigesthomeshow.com

This show offers the opportunity to shop for the latest furniture, lighting, accessories, and art, as well as bath and building products. It is held annually in New York City.

Coverings

coverings.com

Coverings is a trade show dedicated to showcasing natural stone and ceramic tile. It is held in a different U.S. city each year.

Domotex

domotex.de

Domotex is an annual flooring and tile tradeshow in Hanover, Germany.

Dwell on Design

dwellondesign.com

Curated by the editors of *Dwell* magazine, this design show is held twice a year: once in Los Angeles and once in New York.

High Point Market

highpointmarket.org

A semiannual, trade-only home furnishings show held in High Point, North Carolina.

International Builders Show (IBS)

buildersshow.com

This show, hosted by the National Association of Home Builders, is the largest light construction show in the world. Since 2014 the IBS has teamed up with the KBIS to cohost both shows simultaneously in Las Vegas, Nevada, as part of Design and Construction Week.

International Contemporary Furniture Fair (ICFF)

icff.com

The ICFF is a show for both the trade and the general public focusing on contemporary furniture, seating, carpet, flooring, lighting, wall coverings, accessories, textiles, and kitchen and bath fixtures and materials. It is held annually in New York.

International Window Coverings Expo (IWCE)—Vision

wf-vision.com

Also a participant in Design and Construction Week in Las Vegas, the IWCE Vision is an annual show specifically for window coverings.

Kitchen and Bath Industry Show (KBIS)

kbis.com

Showcases the latest trends, technologies, and products in the kitchen and bathroom industry. Held annually in Las Vegas, Nevada, during Design and Construction Week.

Las Vegas Market

lasvegasmarket.com

This show focuses on furniture, home décor, and gifts and is held annually in Las Vegas, Nevada.

NeoCon

neocon.com

North America's largest design exposition for commercial interiors, held annually in Chicago.

Surfaces

surfaces.com

Flooring, stone and tile show held annually in Las Vegas, Nevada.

Resources by Chapter

Chapter Two

Insurance Associations

Independent Insurance Agents & Brokers of America

800-221-7917

independentagent.com

Insurance Information Institute

212-346-5500

iii.org

National Insurance Consumer Helpline

1001 Pennsylvania Avenue, NW

Washington, DC 20004

800-942-4242

consumerservicesguide.org

Chapter 4

Business Plan Resources

ASID

asid.org/content/develop-business-plan

BPlans

bplans.com/interior_design_business_plan/executive_summary_fc.php

Small Business Administration

sba.gov/writing-business-plan

Chapter 5
Business Software and Services

ACT

act.com

ACT is contact management software available for Mac or PC and with an app for iPhone, iPad, and Android.

Designer Advantage

designeradvantage.com

DA provides integrated bookkeeping, billing management, and purchasing services exclusively to the design trade. They manage design businesses and also offer business coaching.

Designer Logic

designerlogic.com

Designer Logic is business software created by design professionals. It can handle proposals, invoicing, and ordering. This software will only run on Windows computers.

Design Manager

designmanager.com

Design Manager is project management and accounting software created specifically for interior designers. Available in Windows-only desktop software or via Cloud-based software, which is available to Mac users.

FreshBooks

freshbooks.com

FreshBooks is an online-only accounting software that allows customers to create invoices, track expenses, and track billable time. It can export reports to Quick-Books. Since it is web-based, FreshBooks is compatible with Mac and PC. It also offers an app for iPhone and Android.

Full Contact

fullcontact.com

Full Contact is an online contact manager; cloud based, so it works with Mac or PC. Business card reader app available for iPhone and Android.

QuickBooks

quickbooks.intuit.com

QuickBooks offers online and desktop software for businesses of all different sizes to handle invoicing, payroll, accepting payments, tracking expenses, and book-keeping. Products are available for Mac, PC, and apps for iPad, iPhone, and Android.

Sage 50

na.sage.com

Sage 50 offers desktop accounting software for small businesses to cover payroll, credit card processing, bill payment, expense tracking, and more. This software is only compatible with computers running Windows.

The Smart Designer

thesmartdesigner.com

DesignSmart is a software system developed for interior design firms. It allows users to create an image library, generate proposals, invoices, and other documents. It is Cloud-based so it runs on Macs or PCs and has an available app for iPhone and iPad.

Studio Webware

studiowebware.com

Studio Webware is online project management and accounting software for the interior design industry. This web-based software will work with Mac operating systems and Windows. They also offer an app for iPhone or iPad.

Studio I.T.

studioitinc.com

Studio I.T. offers different business solutions for the design industry. Their Studio Designer and Studio Showroom software, both for Windows only, give design businesses the accounting tools they need. The new Studio Webware is Cloud based. Studio I.T. also offers web development services.

Chapter 6

Blogging

Blogger

blogger.com

Google's free blogging tool, hosted on blogspot.com, allows users to have multiple blogs through one account. It interfaces with Google's other products, such as Google Docs and Google Analytics.

SquareSpace

squarespace.com

SquareSpace is a website publishing platform that offers an extensive array of style options with a focus on visual imagery and simplicity.

Typepad

typepad.com

Typepad is a blogging service used by many large organizations and media companies to host their blogs.

WordPress

wordpress.org

WordPress is a free web-based software that can be used to create a website or blog.

Email Marketing

Constant Contact

contstantcontact.com

An online marketing toolkit for small businesses, Constant Contact allows users to create email newsletters, surveys, events, Facebook promotions, and more.

iContact

icontact.com

Provides online email marketing services.

MailChimp

mailchimp.com

MailChimp offers a way to manage and optimize email marketing by storing information about website customer activity, targeting emails based on this information, and analyzing effectiveness of messages. It allows users to send marketing emails from mobile devices.

Social Media

Facebook

facebook.com

Facebook allows a small business to connect directly with customers to build relationships through fan pages. Customers can give feedback and spread word about a business by "liking" it.

Instagram

instagram.com

Instagram allows users to quickly take and share photographs. It can also automatically post to Facebook, Twitter, or Tumblr.

LinkedIn

linkedin.com

LinkedIn is a social network focused on professional networking. Use it to connect with others in your field to find professional opportunities.

Pinterest

pinterest.com

Pinterest is a visual bookmarking site that allows users to keep track of ideas and information from around the web, organize it by theme or topic, and share links or ideas. It also acts as a search engine by allowing users to search for particular information.

Twitter

twitter.com

Twitter is an online social media and microblogging website. Users can "tweet" or post photos, videos or links, along with up to 140 characters of text and follow the "tweets" or other users.

Yelp

yelp.com

Yelp is an online business review site that allows users from the general public to write reviews for all kinds of businesses. Users can comment on and share each other's reviews.

YouTube

youtube.com

YouTube is a video sharing website. It is also owned by Google and can be accessed through a Google account. Uploading videos is free and individual users upload most content.

Hootsuite

hootsuite.com

Hootsuite is a social media dashboard that allows users to post to multiple social media accounts at once with one login and schedule future posts. It also provides analytics to measure the impact of messages.

Chapter 9
Hard-Line Window Coverings

Elero USA, Inc.

elerousa.com

800-752-8677

Carries supplies to motorize all hard-lines and soft treatments.

FUA Window Coverings, Ltd.

gotofua.com

888-412-0606

Manufactures an exquisite line of handwoven woods.

Graber

graberblinds.com

877-792-0002

Manufactures shades, blinds, and draperies.

Hunter Douglas

hunterdouglas.com

800-789-0331

Manufactures its own line of hard-line treatments including shades and blinds.

Kirsch

kirsch.com

800-538-6567

Manufactures blinds, shades, and drapery hardware.

Lafayette Venetian Blinds, Inc.

lafvb.com

800-342-5523

Fabricates all major brands of hard-lines as well as fabrics and wallpaper. Also fabricates draperies, bedding, and accessories. Check their "Green"-certified products.

O'Hair Shutters, Ltd.

ohair.com

800-582-2625

Manufactures shutters.

Timber Blind and Shutter

timberblinds.com

877-434-2000

Manufactures wood blinds and fabricates woven woods, cellular shades, shutters, and mini blinds.

Vista Products

vistaproducts.com

800-888-6680

Manufactures its own lines of wood blinds, mini blinds, and shutters. Excellent source.

Chapter 9

Soft Window Treatment, Upholstery & Bedding

ADO

800-845-0918

ado-usa.com

Carries an extensive line of seamless sheers, laces, jacquards, prints, and embroideries.

Fabricut Fabrics

fabricut.com

800-999-8200

Carries drapery and upholstery fabrics.

F. Schumacher and Co.

fschumacher.com

800-523-1200

Manufactures high-end drapery and upholstery fabrics for both residential and contract use.

Lady Ann Fabrics, Inc.

ladyannfabrics.com

800-237-2883

Carries drapery and upholstery fabrics, linings and trims. Offers a custom bedding program.

P. Collins, Ltd. Fabrics/Carolyn Fabrics, Inc.
carolynfabrics.com
336-887-3086 / 336-887-3101
Extensive line of drapery and upholstery fabrics. Also vinyl, outdoor fabrics, trim, and hardware.

Robert Allen Fabrics
robertallendesign.com
800-333-3777
Manufactures drapery and upholstery fabrics. Also has an extensive line of trim, hardware, and shades.

Scroll Fabrics, Inc.
scrollfabrics.com
770-432-7228
The Interior Designer's workroom for quality custom bedcovering products and accessories made with your customers' own fabrics.

Thibaut Wallpapers & Fabrics
thibautdesign.com
800-223-0704
The country's oldest wallpaper manufacturer, Thibaut offers fabrics, wall coverings, and upholstered furniture.

Waverly
waverly.com
A leading manufacturer of various products including fabrics, wall coverings, paint, bedding, window treatments, decorative accessories, and other key products.

Flooring
Anderson Hardwood Floors
andersonfloors.com
864-408-3000
Manufactures hardwood floors.

Armstrong World Industries
armstrong.com
717-397-0611

Manufactures residential and commercial flooring products. Armstrong also has a line of ceiling and cabinet products.

Dash & Albert Rug Company
dashandalbert.com
800-658-5035
Fresh and fun indoor and outdoor carpets, cushions, pillows, and poufs.

Emser Tile and Natural Stone
emser.com
323-650-2000
Manufactures and imports ceramic tile.

Interceramic, Inc.
interceramicusa.com
972-243-4465
Manufactures ceramic tile.

Merida
meridastudio.com
800-345-2200
High-end custom natural-fiber rugs and textiles.

Mohawk Industries
mohawkflooring.com
800-266-4295
Complete flooring source for carpet, hardwood, ceramic, laminate, and vinyl.

Natural Area Rugs
naturalarearugs.com
800-661-7847
Discount natural grass and sisal rugs, custom cut to order.

Shaw Floors
shawfloors.com
800-441-7429
Manufactures carpet. Check their Shaw's "Green Edge" carpets.

Stanton Carpet Corporation

stantoncarpet.com

706-624-9385

Distributes fine-quality carpet and rugs.

S & S Mills

ssmillsinc.com

800-241-4013

Manufactures carpet.

Unique Carpets, Ltd.

uniquecarpetsltd.com

800-547-8266

Manufactures carpet. Large selection of wool and sisal carpets.

Wallpaper

Brewster Wallcoverings

brewsterwallcovering.com

800-366-1700

Wallpapers, murals and window films.

Blue Mountain Wall-covering

866-563-9872

BLMTN.com

Wallpapers.

Customized Walls

800-425-9959

customizedwalls.com

Customizable and removable wall coverings.

Graham & Brown

grahambrown.com/us

800-554-0887

Designer wallpaper, wall art, and paintable Superfresco textured vinyl products.

Thibaut Wallpapers & Fabrics

thibautdesign.com

800-223-0704

The country's oldest wallpaper manufacturer, Thibaut offers fabrics, wall coverings, and upholstered furniture.

York Wallcoverings
yorkwall.com
1-800-375-YORK (9675)
Wallpapers from brands such as Candice Olsen, Waverly and Walt Disney.

Miscellaneous
DreamDraper
dreamdraper.com
866-563-7326
Premier design and visualization system for the interior design industry, specializing in window treatments.

Fabric Services
fabriclaminating.com
877-372-2620
Carries various laminated fabrics. Also custom laminates fabrics.

M'Fay Patterns
mfay.com
704-795-9888
Extensive line of drapery patterns.

Soft-Tex Manufacturing
soft-tex.com
800-366-2324
Manufactures pillows, pillow forms, mattress pads, toppers, comforters, blankets, memory foam, and bulk fiber.

Vista Window Film
vista-films.com
800-345-6088
Manufactures protective window film.

Rendering and Floorplan Software
Home Designer 2015 from Chief Architect
homedesignersoftware.com

This downloadable software is compatible with both Mac and PC. It provides both architectural and interior design options.

Icovia Space Planner

icovia.com

Room planning tools in both 2D and 3D. The software is compatible with both Mac and PC and apps are available for iPad.

Live Interior 3D Pro

belightsoft.com/products/liveinterior/proversion.php

An interior and home design tool with a variety of editing and output options. Compatible with both Mac and PC. Apps available for iPhone and Android.

Minutes Matter

minutesmatter.com

The studio graphic design software is available in both desktop and online versions. Provides custom forms to help a designer measure a job, work up a bid, or create work orders. Compatible with Mac, PC and iPad.

Room sketcher

roomsketcher.com

Roomsketcher offers a free version and a professional version. Both versions allow users to create 3D floor plans and home designs. Compatible with Mac and PC.

Sketch

sketchup.com

Sketchup is a 3D modeling software that is compatible with both Macs and computers on Windows operating systems. There is also an app for iPhone and Android.

Green Seal

greenseal.org

Green Seal is a nonprofit organization that develops sustainability standards for products, services and companies, including those related to interior design. This is a good resource for information on eco-friendly paint and construction materials.

The Home.com

thehome.com

This site, run by Ellen Gefen, features articles and videos on the latest furniture and design trends, as well as ideas and quick tips.

Homeowners Marketing Services, Inc.

homeownersmarketingservices.com

Mailing lists and other data compiled about new homeowners in specific geographic areas. Increase sales by reaching new homeowners first.

Kitchen Design Network

kitchendesignnetwork.com

A community of designers exploring kitchen design and the culture of kitchens worldwide. They offer an annual schedule of kitchen design workshops nation-wide.

Chapter 10
Business and Sales Development
Design Biz Blueprint

designbizblueprint.com

Terri Taylor

Coaching and mentoring programs on the business of design including contracts, client relationships, marketing and money issues.

Design Success University

designsuccessu.com

Gail Doby and Erin Wier

Interior design business coaching, marketing, and client acquisition.

Interior Design Camp

designcamp.com

Lori Dennis and Kelli Ellis

Design Camps take place during major trade shows such as the Las Vegas Market and include showroom tours, well-known industry speakers and social events.

National Association of Women Business Owners (NAWBO)

nawbo.org

800-556-2926

Nika Stewart

nikastewart.com

Nika Stewart provides expert advice in marketing through social media and increased online visibility for designers and entrepreneurs.

Tobi Fairley's Designer MBA

tobifairley.com/events/designer-mba/

Tobi Fairley

Designer MBA is a two-day session in business education for design professionals run by designer Tobi Fairley. Tobi covers topics such as fees, staffing, and marketing.

Appendix B: Solutions to Practice Problems

Answers to the practice questions on pages 160–65.

1. $1,188.48. See the surcharge for shades under 12".
2. $80.10 for the regular-priced shade. $102.60 for two shades on one headrail. See the surcharge listed at the bottom of the price chart and add it to the retail before you deduct your discounts.
3. $67.95. Again, remember to figure in your surcharge.
4. $83.04. No additional charge for controls change. See note at bottom of price chart.
5. $103.95. Add a 50-percent surcharge for a bottom-up shade. See note on price chart.
6. The best application for this window is to use three mini blinds on one headrail. Remember, there is a $145 surcharge for this feature.
7. $223.89. To increase energy efficiency, use insert channels on the vertical blinds.
8. $605.95.
9. $100.10.
10. $463.12.
11. $518.10.
12. King-size throw fabric is $162.60. Fabric for the shams $53.80 and pillows $35.60. The labor is $140. Total for all is: $468
13. The carpet will cost $333 and the tile will cost $406.56. Don't forget to add 10% for a contingency.
14. The wallpaper will cost $325, and you will need six border rolls (remember to round up).

Index

About the Editor

Linda Merrill is an award-winning interior designer with an expertise in the fields of interior design, media communications, and marketing. A lifelong passion for creating beautiful—and livable—spaces combined with a savvy business mind has brought her design work and writing to a national and international audience. Since 2002, Linda has offered her interior design and decorating services throughout New England and virtually worldwide. Linda is a sought-after writer and voice in the field of interior design and not only publishes her own popular blog, Surroundings, but is a contributing writer to other media outlets. She is also founder and moderator of the popular podcast *The Skirted Round-table*. Her website is www.LindaMerrill.com.